DISCARD

Understanding the Arsonist:
From Assessment to Confession

Dian L. Williams, Ph.D., RN, CLNC, DF-IAFN

®Lawyers & Judges
Publishing Company, Inc.
Tucson, Arizona

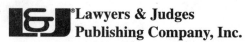

Lawyers & Judges Publishing Company, Inc.

P.O. Box 30040 • Tucson, AZ 85751-0040
(800) 209-7109 • FAX (800) 330-8795
e-mail: sales@lawyersandjudges.com

Williams, Dian L.
 Understanding the arsonist : from assessment to confession / Dian L. Williams.
  p. cm.
 Includes bibliographical references.
 ISBN 1-930056-58-3 (pbk.)
 1. Arson--Psychological aspects. 2. Pyromania--Psychological aspects. I. Title.
RC569.5.P9W554 2005
364.16'4--dc22

                    2005000222

ISBN 1-930056-58-3
Printed in the United States of America
10 9 8 7 6 5 4 3 2 1

online
www.lawyersandjudges.com

Contents

Acknowledgments

I wish to express my heartfelt appreciation to my family, friends, colleagues, professional associates, and the myriad arson and police investigators who have encouraged and supported this research over the years here in the United States as well as in the United Kingdom.

First and foremost, I am indebted to my daughter, Romy Riddick, for providing me with her infinite skills as a researcher. She will never know how her tedious examination of the 310 cases in the sample used for this textbook brought me the peace of mind it did. Romy determined every variable that was identified, reviewing all evaluations and supportive documentation on each case, reading thousands of pages of material in her efforts. I was able to speak with complete assurance about our data because of her efforts. She is a wonderful addition to our team.

I owe an enormous debt of gratitude to two outstanding interview specialists, Dana Crall and Curtis Watkins, who did 99 percent of the evaluation work over the last year so I could finish writing this book. They will never know how comforted I was because they were always available to respond to evaluation requests. I am also in debt to Sandy Carl, the Center for Arson Research office manager, who always thought I should write a book about what we do. Her organizational skills keep us focused and she serves to remind us what goes into a good evaluation, along with making sure we meet our various deadlines.

I am deeply indebted to Mary Ellen Donnelly, master copy editor, close friend, and the only person who read every word of the text before it made its way to the publisher. Her eye for detail was truly amazing, and she kept me focused. Her criticisms were always kind, even though she was disappointed that I didn't begin the book with, "It was a dark and stormy night."

There are few words that could adequately express my gratitude at having our computer wizard, Eric Santiago, available to minister to the various pieces of equipment used to write this text. Eric was a calm voice of reason during every panicked phone call, day or night, about lost data or frozen screens and truly, this book would not have happened without him.

There are four members of the fire service who have particularly supported my work over the years: Andy Braig of New Jersey, John Lattomus of Delaware, and Carl Collum and Mike Logan of Texas. They are superior fire investigators who recognized early in their careers that there are multiple reasons for setting fires and that those reasons have investigative importance. We shared stories, ideas, and experiences, and they never held it against me that I was not a member of the fire service. What I know about actual fire scene investigation comes from them and what I don't know isn't their fault. No acknowledgement would be complete without mentioning Timothy G. Huff, retired FBI analyst, who was (and is) a supportive research colleague and a gentleman of wisdom and intellect. He believed in our findings and offered me encouragement over the years.

As I look back over the past twenty years, I want to extend my gratitude to those individuals who were there during the early days of the Center: Norma Lindbloom who did all our billing and final edits of the evaluations; Justin Williams, Brian McGinley, Keith Lowack, Jamie Cassium, Larry Lukin, and Mary Jo Keenan (one of the world's best psychiatric nurses), who did evaluations with me, figuring out the variables that made sense and that had the potential to identify risk for continued firesetting. They will never know how much I appreciated their intelligence, dedication, and hard work. Ed Quinn, who has long offered me business advice and accompanied me to many a meeting over the years, has been invaluable as a close friend and business mentor. I am also grateful to my colleague and friend, Paul Clements, whose expertise in counseling children exposed to traumatic events has been of invaluable help to our research. His energy and enthusiasm have been a source of vicarious comfort and inspiration.

Finally, I want to thank my publisher, Steve Weintraub, for approaching me with the idea for this textbook and being so understanding about my pleas for extensions!

Dedication

This text is dedicated to my daughter Romy and son-in-law, Derek, and to my son, Justin, and daughter-in-law Tanya, for their unfailing support and love. They are wonderful people and awesome parents.

It is also dedicated to my grandchildren Jordan, Austin, Kory, Chase, and Summer who remind me of how childhood should look after I have spent a day interviewing early childhood firesetters. May they always walk in love.

Finally, the text is dedicated to my sister, Adrian, who has always been there for me and is proud of me as I am proud of her and to my mother, Eve Parkinson, who took the news of this undertaking in stride and who believed I had something to say. Thank you for your support and love.

I also dedicate this text to the memory of my stepfather, Ed Parkinson, the last real John Wayne.

Chapter 1

An Overview of Firesetting

Joey, age 13, leaves his home during the middle of the night through his bedroom window, something his parents do not know. While out and about, Joe sets fires at various locations-dumpsters, back porches, bushes-it does not matter. At his own count, Joey has set "about 200 fires since I was a little kid." His fires have gotten bigger and more of them are being set to occupied homes, near the front or back door. He says "Setting fires really gets my anger out. I feel great after it; like I have no problems."

Arson is a crime defined as "any willful or malicious burning or attempt to burn, with or without intent to defraud, a dwelling, house, public building, motor vehicle or aircraft, or personal property of another" (FBI, 2000, p.54). The primary sources of information on arson are found within the Uniform Crime Report (UCR) produced yearly by the U.S. Department of Justice and the National Fire Protection Association (NFPA). Arson was not added to the UCR until 1979, according to Territo, Halsted, and Bromley (2004). The UCR excludes fires of unknown or suspicious origin while the NFPA reports only structure fires.

Another source of crime data, the National Crime Victimization Survey (NCVS), is an attempt by the Department of Justice to assess the crimes not reported to the police. The NCVS surveys approximately 50,000 households and collects data on personal and household crimes. Although the UCR reports that a property crime (such as arson) occurs every three seconds in the United States, the NCVS does not collect victimization data on unreported, deliberately set fires (Robinson, 2002).

1

Use of official statistics to understand the scope of criminal behavior is problematic because it reflects only crimes known to the police. Because of the dual investigative roles of police and fire service departments, police officers do not report some fires identified by fire investigators as arson even though arson is a felony in all jurisdictions. Generally, arson charges reflect the level of danger or damage involved in the crime. An occupied dwelling fire results in first-degree arson, an unoccupied dwelling results in second-degree arson and a fire to an unoccupied dwelling, owned by the arsonist and burned for the purposes of insurance fraud, brings a third-degree arson charge (Inciardi, 1996). Overall, however, arson is underreported and undercounted, according to Jackson (1988).

Arson reports found in the UCR have a number of unique characteristics. UCR reporting guidelines preclude the inclusion of any fires not officially determined as intentionally set, even if arson is strongly suspected. This is of particular significance when fires are set by youth because many cases of deliberate firesetting by children and adolescents are not reported (Jackson, 1988). Firesetting behavior in youth poses a particular problem for the juvenile justice and mental health systems. Youngsters who set fires are frequently excused for their behavior through an often misguided perception that they were "playing with matches" or were unaware of the danger. Adolescents who set fires are generally perceived as delinquent and their firesetting behavior is regarded as symptomatic of antisocial conduct (Jacobson, 1985).

The primary sources for arson statistics reveal that the annual clearance rate for arson is about 15 percent (FBI, 1997) and that more than 50 percent are set by youth under age eighteen years. Adler, et al. (1994) recognizes a general acknowledgement that only a small portion of fires set by youth are ever reported, perhaps fewer than 10 percent. Approximately 1,000 citizens and 120 members of the fire service are killed yearly in arson fires while 30,000 civilians and 4,000 firefighters are injured (Brady, 1983). Males account for 85.3 percent and females account for 14.7 percent of all arrests for arson according to the FBI (1994). Structures are the most frequent targets of arsonists at 52 percent while vehicle and other moving property fires represent 25 percent of set fire targets (Karter, 1994).

Despite the fact that over $1 billion is lost in property damage and hundreds of people are killed yearly in deliberately set fires, official reporting of arson data to the UCR did not begin until 1979, as noted earlier.

An indication of the lack of reliability of arson statistics can be found in the arson fires reported to the UCR program in 2001. The UCR received crime reports from more than 16,000 law enforcement agencies during that year; of that number, there were 12,242 arson reports (FBI, Uniform Crime Reports, 2001). The UCR program has not been successful in the integration of arson statistics into its yearly index of crime. Schmalleger (2004) observes that the arson data from the UCR does not generally include information on amount or cost of damage and provides no information on property ownership. The lack of data gathering on the federal level until 1979, along with the general lack of information on the crime itself, has led to an incomplete historical perspective on arson in the United States.

Statistics from the UCR for 2001 indicate that there were 29,088 reports of arson fires to dwellings or structures and 22,381 reports of arson fires to vehicles. The average dollar loss per fire was estimated at $11,098 with the national estimated dollar loss from arson fires at approximately $1 billion. Overall, the clearance rate for arson cases is at 16 percent nationally (Schmalleger, 2004). Figures available for 1997 (Snyder, 1999) reveal that there were 20,000 arrests for arson in that year and that 50 percent of the arrestees were under eighteen years of age. Adolescent males made up 89 percent of the arrests and 79 percent of the population were white males while youth under age fifteen represented 67 percent of the total arrests. Youth, ages twelve and under, were involved in 35 percent of the total number of all arson arrests. Many juvenile firesetters, especially those below the age of twelve, are diverted into mental health facilities rather than detention facilities. As a result, the Federal Emergency Management Agency (FEMA) believes that the real incidence of juvenile firesetting is well above the estimated 50 percent in the official FBI database (FBI, 1997).

The Historical Perspective on Firesetting Research

A major shortcoming of arson studies has been a lack of universality. Arsonists have been studied in unrepresentative samples, such as prisoners convicted of arson or mentally ill offenders. Those findings were then applied to all arsonists, including children and adolescents. Blumberg (1981) stated, "Part of the problem with the studies of firesetters is the result of intrinsic difficulties, such as inadequate design, biased sampling, unreliable subjects and misinterpretation of conclusions." (p. 255). Arson classification systems historically mix behavior, motives and offender characteristics while reflecting arson as a legal term. The result has been one of confusion with contradictory studies and theories based on poor sampling and a less than sound database (Barker, 1994).

The first recorded attempts to understand the motivation for firesetting began in Germany in the early nineteenth century. German scientists proposed that fires were set almost exclusively by mentally retarded females suffering from severe menstrual problems and abnormal sexual development. Marco, a French scientist, studied arsonists in 1833 and concluded that certain individuals suffered from an irresistible urge to set fires. Marco termed these arsonists pyromaniacs, a word still in use today (Geller, 1992).

A Closer Look at Pyromania

Pyromania is found in the American Psychiatric Association's *Diagnostic and Statistical Manual of Mental Disorders-IV* (1994) as the diagnostic classification, for individuals who "receive pleasure, gratification or relief when setting fires." (p. 615). A significant number of fire investigators, forensic specialists and other scientific researchers take exception to the definition of pyromania and to its use, overall. Sapsford, Banks, and Smith (1978) observed that there is a lack of understanding about the etiology of arson through a concentration on pyromania by the psychiatric community. The authors note, "Research tends to have been confined to special security hospitals and institutions for the mentally ill, focusing on the most psychiatrically disturbed offenders." (p. 247). Huff, Gary and Icove (1997) identified three basic philosophies of pyromania that have existed since the nineteenth century. They include a view that pyromania is a mental illness; another view holds that pyromania is a behavior of a more general mental illness or a criminal act; and the third view is that no conclusion could be drawn at all about the behavior.

Prior to the 1970s, most of the research into firesetting behavior supported the idea of arson as an irresistible impulse experienced by males unable to control their behavior. Freud, in a monograph published in 1932, stated that males set fires as a symbolic act that expressed personally unacceptable sexual desires. He further posited that arsonists urinated on their fires as a symbolic manifestation of a sexual struggle, "In order to possess himself of fire, it was necessary for man to renounce the homosexually tinged desire to extinguish it by a stream of urine." (pp 406-407).

Lewis and Yarnell (1951), in a study still referenced today, supported Freud's theory of the sexually motivated arsonist as suffering from irresistible impulses to set fires. Studying the prison records of 1,145 adult male incarcerated offenders, Lewis and Yarnell concluded that arsonists were sexually repressed males who experienced the impulse to set fires and masturbated at their fire scenes. Pisani, writing in 1995, observed that the Lewis and Yarnell study was scientifically unsound because they never clearly revealed their data sources and how many of their sample had actually ever set fires. Pisani also noted that the study failed to use a control group and that no attempt was made by the authors to define "arson tendencies." Lewis and Yarnell stated in the conclusion of their study, "No complete intensive analysis can be made of such a group and, in attempting the analysis, we have had to restrict ourselves to the relatively few records where we were able to obtain complete information." (p. 30).

The initial *Diagnostic and Statistical Manual* (DSM), published in 1952, reflected the conclusions drawn by the Lewis and Yarnell study about the motivation of arsonists. Huff, Gary and Icove (1997) commented that the definition of pyromania came under criticism because it lacked statistical validation. Since that seminal description in the DSM of 1952, the professional psychiatric community has continued to struggle with the definition of pyromania and possible motivations for firesetting behavior. One great stumbling block placed in the way of understanding deliberate firesetting is in the differences in definitions used by mental health providers, criminal justice investigators, and the legal community to describe the same behavior. The current version of the diagnostic manual, DSM-IV, describes pyromania as an impulse control disorder characterized by "...a fascination with, interest in, curiosity about, or attraction to fire and its situational contexts"...(p. 614). The manual goes on to say that firesetting behavior in children is rare despite the acknowledgement that over 40 percent of those arrested for arson offenses are under age eighteen. The DSM-IV observes "there are insufficient data to establish a typical age of onset of pyromania. The relationship between fire setting in childhood and pyromania in adulthood has not been documented." (p. 614). Despite the lack of an established relationship, children and adolescents with firesetting behavior frequently carry the diagnosis of pyromania.

Huff, Gary and Icove (1997) experienced the same phenomenon, as did this writer, while researching motivation into firesetting behavior—an inability to replicate the findings of Lewis and Yarnell (1951) or the claims in the DSM-IV. The manual offers exclusionary diagnostic criteria for the diagnosis of pyromania. In effect, the diagnosis excludes an arsonist who sets fires for "monetary gain, as an expression of sociopolitical ideology, to conceal criminal activity, to express anger or vengeance, to improve one's living circumstances, in response to a delusion or hallucination, or as a result of impaired judgment (e.g., in dementia, mental retardation, substance intoxication)" (p. 615). Huff et al. mention that they failed to find any arsonist in face-to-face interviews with eighty-one convicted arson offenders who met the criteria for pyromania. Instead, when questioned about their motives for setting fires, the subjects identified feelings of anger (33 percent), frustration (6 percent), sad (3.7 percent), afraid (8.6 percent), happy (9.9 percent), no particular feelings (9.9 percent) and a combination of feelings (28 percent) (p. 6). My own experience in interviewing hundreds of firesetters from early childhood through adult life replicates that of Huff, Gary, and Icove; few active firesetters of any age fit into the diagnostic criteria for pyromania.

Thurber and Dahmes (1999), writing in the text *Child and Adolescent Psychological Disorders*, discuss the DSM classification of "impulse control disorders"; pyromania being one of them. This text discusses only the authors' comments relative to pyromania and directs the reader to the chapter found in the cited work by Thurber and Dahmes for a fuller account of impulse disorders, overall. The writers note that the literature available on firesetting behavior in youth does not correspond with the criteria for pyromania in the DSM-IV or the ICD-10 (*International Classification of Diseases*). Thurber and Dahmes observe that certain changes were made to the most recent editions of both manuals. The "ICD-10 substitutes 'preoccupation' for 'fascination' and 'curiosity' and cites post event 'intense excitement' (p. 448). The DSM-IV now includes exclusionary criteria for depression, conduct disorder and antisocial personality disorder. Thurber and Dahmes state, citing an American Psychiatric Association study of 1994, that no cases of pyromania have been reported in the Unites States since 1970. This is somewhat bemusing, as pyromania continues to be a fairly popular diagnosis for firesetters (adult and youth) in mental health facilities and criminal justice agencies throughout the country.

The authors, Thurber and Dahmes, (1999) note that little research has been conducted to date on youth who have set fires and have the requisite pre-fire tension and arousal state and the post fire gratification or relief. They posit that studies have neglected these essential criteria of the pyromania diagnosis or are simply unable to identify them in the subjective reports of the firesetters studied. In sum, Thurber and Dahmes wonder about the diagnostic validity of impulse disorders overall and the diagnosis of pyromania specifically. The work by Huff, Gary and Icove (1997) agree with the observations by Thurber and Dahmes, noting that none of the identified arsonists in their study met the diagnostic criteria of the DSM-IV and all fell under the exclusionary criteria, especially when motivation is considered.

A Review of Studies on Motivation: Trends and Concepts

Classification of firesetters by motivation has always been a particular problem for research into the behavior. Vreeland and Waller (1979) found classification systems to be arbitrary and inconsistent. In fact, some firesetters are classified by motive (such as jealousy or fraud) some are sorted by gender and age (such as female adolescents) while others are identified by behavior or diagnostic symptoms (such as anger or delusions). The result of such a mix of classification systems, when considered along with the exclusionary criteria for pyromania found in the DSM-IV, is a confusion of legal and psychiatric concepts and poorly conceived research. The writer feels strongly that a conflict between mental health and criminal justice manifests itself quite strongly in the study of firesetting behavior.

Siegel (2003) states that there are several motives for arson. "Adult arsonists may be motivated by severe emotional turmoil. Some psychologists view fire starting as a function of a disturbed personality." (p. 382), something that argues the behavior as an emotional, not criminal act. Siegel also notes that arsonists are alleged to experience sexual pleasure from firesetting and observation of the destructive nature of their acts, a long-standing conclusion drawn from the earlier work of Freud (1932) and Lewis and Yarnell (1951).

Geller (1992) believed that many research designs in the study of firesetting were seriously flawed because of the complexity of the task. He suggested that a clearer method of classification might be found if researchers categorized behavior, not individuals. Geller developed his own arson classification system by dividing motivation for firesetting into four broad categories: unassociated with psychobiologic disorders, associated with mental disorders, juvenile and associated with medical or neurological disorders. Unfortunately, Geller's classification continued to mix apples and oranges by producing a list of categories that includes diagnoses (such as AIDS dementia), mental status findings (delusions of thought), motive (such as revenge) and age (juvenile). Williams (1998) described several other typologies of arson developed by research into the behavior by comparing the classification systems of Geller (1992), to that of Magee (1933), Swaffer and Hollin (1995), Inciardi (1996) and Ravateheino (1989). It is noted that these attempts at classifying arsonists relate to adult firesetters; other classification systems have been developed for juveniles and will be described elsewhere in this text. Table 1.1 describes a number of classification systems.

Table 1.1
Arson Typologies

Researchers	Classification Categories
Magee	Pathological Pyromaniacs and Non-Pathological for Profit
Harris & Rice (1961)	Psychotic Under-Assertive Multi-Firesetter and Criminal
Swaffer & Hollin (1995)	Revenge, Crime Concealment, Self-Injury, Peer Pressure, Denial, and Experimental
Inciardi (1996)	Revenge, Excitement, Institutionalized, Insurance Claim, Act of Concealment
Ravateheino (1989)	Insurance Fraud, Revenge, Jealousy, Hatred, Envy, Grudge, Sensation, Alcoholic and Mental Patients, Temporarily Disturbed, Vandalism, Pyromaniacs, and Children Under Fifteen

Barker (1994) called for an arson classification system that would include motivation along with a multi-axial description of the behavior. She believes such a classification system would be of benefit in the development of intervention strategies and the ability to assess risk. It is clear that attempts at classifying the motivation of firesetters to date has generally resulted in confusion and misinformation.

Arson as Sexually Deviant Symbolism

In 1932, Freud (1932) wrote a monograph on arsonists that changed the way firesetting was perceived and it remains a critical influence today. Freud studied four male firesetters in the course of his analytic practice and arrived at certain conclusions that he applied rather sweepingly to all arsonists. He determined that arsonists were psychosexually immature (and by inference, homosexual in inclination) males who set fires as an act of sexual symbolism. Freud proposed that certain men set fires to represent the powerful phallus as manifested by flames. Further, Freud suggested that these men then urinated on the fires they created as a symbolic expression of their struggle with homosexuality. He stated, "In order to possess himself of fire, it was necessary for man to renounce the homosexually tinged desire to extinguish it by a stream of urine." (pp. 406-407). Gaynor and Hatcher (1987) observed that Freud's theory of fire and sexual desire lent credibility to the mythic association, still reflected in the literature of today (Williams, 1998).

Lewis and Yarnell (1951), writing in a highly popular study of arsonists still cited today, supported Freud's premise on arson as a sexually motivated crime. After studying the prison records of over 1,000 offenders with arson histories or "arson tendencies," Lewis and Yarnell concluded that arsonists were psychosexually repressed males who masturbated to orgasm at fire scenes. Critics of the Lewis and Yarnell study, such as Pisani (1995), observe that, while the research contained in the study was scientifically unsound, it continues to be cited as a credible resource.

Inciardi (1970) studied 138 white male paroled arsonists and found results that supported Freud's work of 1932. Although Inciardi divided his arson subjects into six subgroups (revenge, excitement, mental deficit, fraud, vandalism and as a red herring), he posited that all the subtypes were inclined towards sexual perversion, had low intelligence and functioned as social outcasts. Halleck (1967), while writing about conscious sexual motivation and crime wrote, "One crime which is often accompanied by conscious sexual gratification is arson. Setting and putting out fires is a not uncommon masturbation fantasy of some disturbed persons. A sizeable percentage of arsonists report great sexual arousal in starting a fire, watching a building burn or in watching firemen extinguish a blaze." "...The arsonist is believed to be responding to an unconscious fantasy of obtaining gratification through urinating on the fire." (p. 194). Halleck goes on to note that although the theory might seem far-fetched to those dubious about the value of psychoanalytic theory, he finds that ... "many individuals who are arsonists and who experience some sexual gratification through setting fires are also people who experienced enuresis in their earlier lives" (p. 194). Incidentally, in 1997, the Center for Arson Research abandoned data collection on enuretic behavior after more than twelve years of gathering the information, having found no evidence of a relationship between enuresis and firesetting that was also not reflective of the general population of non-firesetting bed-wetters.

MacDonald (1977) supported the belief that arsonists are sexually deviant males in a text entitled *Bombers and Firesetters*. He posited that arsonists set fires as an acknowledgement that they were impotent without fire. He also claimed that arsonists collected women's underwear at fire scenes because they were transvestites. A later study by Sakheim, Vigdor, Gordon, and Helprin (1885) looked at fifteen juvenile firesetters and fifteen non-firesetter juveniles. They found that the firesetter group had weak ego structures and set fires for intense sexual excitement. Such studies have served to reinforce the concept of the arsonist as a bizarre sex offender. A study by Quinsey, Chaplin, and Unfold (1989) however, found little evidence that arsonists are motivated by psychosexual excitement. Williams (2004) in an expanded study of 310 firesetters was unable to identify a psychosexual link as a primary behavioral motivator.

Siegel (2004) notes that there are several reasons for arson and that one of them is alleged sexual excitement secondary to starting fires and observing the results. Siegel states, "Although some arsonists may be aroused sexually by their activities, there is little evidence that most arsonists are psychosexually motivated" (p. 390). A study by Sapp, Huff, Gary and Icove (1994) offers the following observation, "Offenders motivated by excitement include seekers of thrills, attention, recognition and rarely, but importantly, sexual gratification. The stereotypical arsonist who sets fires for sexual gratification is quite rare" (p. 7).

Arson as an Expression of Aggression

During the later part of the 1960s and during the decade of the 1970s, research interest into firesetting behavior shifted away from arson as motivated by sexual deviance to arson as an act of indirect aggression. A study by McKerraccher and Dacre (1966) compared thirty adult male arsonists to 147 adult non-arson offenders in a forensic psychiatric setting and suggested that arsonists were influenced by feelings of aggression. In a study conducted in 1972, Wolford found that arsonists, in general, were men who were unable to express anger directly to others. His work caused him challenge the narrow legal definition of arson because of the many reasons arsonists had for setting fires (Williams, 1999). Research conducted by Bandura and Waller (1959) supported Wolford's earlier work; they posited that anxiety and aggression were closely linked in children. Vreeland and Waller analyzed firesetting behavior and concluded that firesetters were unable to directly confront the object of their anger and displaced their feelings onto aggression against property (1979). Other studies have supported the concept of arson as an act of aggression and anger. A study of fifteen arsonists in Finland found that 70 percent of the cohort self-identified an inability to directly express anger to others (Rasnen, Puumalainen, Janhonen, and Vaisanen,1996).

The concept of aggression is an important one when attempting to understand the act of deliberate firesetting. Bandura (1973) proposed that aggression and violence are learned in the same way as any other behavior—through something he called observational learning. Bandura believes that all social behavior is communicated through examples provided by the family, the cultural background of the individual, and mass media. Adler, Mueller, and Laufer (1998) mention that we learn through trial and error, based on the rewards and punishments we receive from our behavior. If accepted as true, by extension, certain firesetters have learned that a direct expression of anger carries few rewards, but indirect expression brings positives of some kind. Subsequent chapters of this text will discuss arson as an expression of anger and aggression more comprehensively.

Juvenile Firesetters

By the mid-1980s, interest in firesetting shifted away from the psychoanalytic attempt to explain arson into a closer look at the impact of the environment on conduct. Social scientists, such as Gaynor and Hatcher (1987) and Vreeland and Waller (1979), posited that firesetting, aggression and constricted emotional expression were learned childhood behaviors. Research into the dynamics of firesetting behavior began to focus on youth and their social learning environment. Sociologists, such as Eysenck (1977), supported the concept of learning theory which proposes that all behavior, including aberrant conduct, is learned through direct observation of important role models. According to Siegel (2004), many criminologists believe that individual socialization is the key to criminality, overall. A basic concept of such social process theories is that all individuals have the potential for criminal behavior. If we accept this as a given, it becomes of great importance to determine the reasons that lead some people to become firesetters while some others turn to other criminal acts and still others commit no crime at all.

It seems clear that youth who grow up in violence-plagued environments or in homes where there is little love and emotional support are more susceptible to crime and delinquency than youth who live in emotional comfort, even in a high-crime community. Certain family factors, such as inconsistent discipline, poor supervision by a responsible adult, and parents who are substance abusers or who have a major mental illness influence the risk for delinquency (Johnson, Su, Gerstein, and Hoffman, 1995). Straus (1991) notes that children who receive even a small amount of physical punishment may be more likely to use violence themselves. Arrigo (2000) observes that children who grow up in homes where they are exposed to trauma suffer from psychological, biological and social repercussions. The Center for Arson Research finds that approximately 46 percent of the total population of firesetters report physical abuse during childhood and adolescence.

A small study conducted by Macht and Mack in 1968 studied four adolescents, three males and one female, and concluded that their firesetting caused extreme sexual excitement and destructive fantasies. All four of the subjects had fathers who had some connection to the fire service, leading the researchers to conclude that firesetting was an attempt to bond with their fathers. Macht and Mack theorized that role modeling by significant adults influenced the onset of firesetting in children (Williams, 1998). An ongoing study by the Center for Arson Research has not been able to find more than an occasional associative link between firesetting behavior and the father's work. Fineman (1980) and Gaynor and Hatcher (1987) supported the premise of Macht and Mack's study. They posited that family background, methods of reward and punishment and environmental conditions predisposed some youth to firesetting behavior.

Demographics of Youthful Firesetters

There are certain demographic similarities found in youthful firesetters. Heath et al. (1985) noted that firesetters were more likely than non-firesetters to have conduct disordered behavior while Kuhnley et al. (1982) observed that firesetters were more likely than non-firesetters to carry diagnoses of attention deficit hyperactive disorder. Heath et al. (1985) found that approximately 90 percent of firesetters are male. A study by Wooden and Berkley (1984) suggested that juvenile firesetters are disproportionately middle-class Caucasian males; however, Pisani (1995) referred to that study as suffering from erroneous methodology.

A study of 173 referrals made in 1995 to the Fire Watch Intervention Program in Camden County, NJ of youthful firesetters determined that 85.9 percent of their subjects were male while 14.1 percent were female. The majority of the referrals were in the pre-adolescent age range, came from single parent families and had histories of learning disabilities and impulsive behavior (Braig and Whelan, 1995). The writer suggests that, in her experience, the findings of the Camden County program replicate findings of the demographics of like programs throughout the country.

Juvenile firesetters represented about half of all arson arrests in 2001, according to the FBI (UCR, 2001). In that same year, 32 percent of all those arrested for arson were age fifteen or younger. Data released by FEMA for 1998, indicate that youth started 67,490 fires that caused 232 deaths and 1,805 injuries along with $234 million in property damage. The amount of damage and destruction caused by juvenile firesetters is staggering. Overall, youth who set deliberate fires and who are arrested for their conduct are regarded as delinquent by the juvenile justice system. According to Jensen and Rojek (1992) the National Center for Juvenile Justice estimates that one third of all youth in the United States will acquire an arrest record by the time of his or her eighteenth birthday.

Intellect

Most firesetters appear to fall within the normal range of intelligence, according to Kuhnley et al., (1982); Jacobson, (1985). This finding supports other studies on the relationship between intelligence and firesetting. Showers and Pickrell (1987) found no differences between juvenile firesetters and non-firesetters on the basis of intellect or school performance. An earlier study by Lewis and Yarnell in 1952 found that 111 of 238 children studied because they set fires were unable to function at an appropriate intellectual level in school and set revenge fires as a result. The same study concluded that mentally retarded youth set no fires until after the age of sixteen when they posed a threat to society. Power (1969) posited that firesetters with low IQ's were disproportionately represented in research literature because they were more easily arrested than firesetters with normal intellects. The Center for Arson Research supports the view that most firesetters fall within the normal range of intellect although they appear to disproportionately receive special education services, often associated with learning disabilities and asocial conduct.

Of scholarly interest are studies conducted on the relationship between delinquency and certain other variables, including social class and intellectual skills. Reiss and Rhodes (1961) studied the court records of 9,200 white schoolboys in Tennessee and found that IQ was more closely related to delinquency than to social class. Another study by Hirschi and Hindelang (1977) concluded that a low IQ is more important in crime prediction than other variables such as race or social class and that students with low IQ's do poorly in school and tend to drop out, increasing their risk for committing acts of delinquency. Wilson and Herrnstein (1985) supported that view, agreeing that there was an indirect link between poor school performance and low intelligence because lack of success academically serves to enhance criminal conduct. However, a study by Denno (1985) of 800 children from birth to age seventeen could not find a direct relationship between delinquent conduct and intelligence. In fact, Akers (1997) says that little empirical evidence exists to support the perception that there is a link between low IQ levels and delinquency.

Family Life

Family life may be regarded as a microsystem and families with dysfunctional children may be viewed as suffering from disturbed microsystems. Inadequate patterns of communication found in some families make it virtually impossible to communicate socially acceptable values, ideals and concepts to children (Williams, 1999). The inability to provide a climate for the delivery of nurturing messages is considered conducive to the development of deviant behavior and mental illness in children (Papalia and Olds, 1995). According to Gaines, Kaune, and Miller (2001) fifteen of every 1,000 American children were confirmed by child protective services as suffering from abuse and/or neglect in 1997. It seems clear that children who grow up in homes where exposure to violence or neglect experience a variety of physical, emotional and mental health problems.

A study by Widom (1989) reviewed the arrest rates of adults charged with crimes of violence who had experienced abuse or neglect as children. His conclusions led him to determine that arrestees in the study, who were sexually abused as children, were slightly less likely to commit a violent offense while those who were physically abused were slightly more likely to commit a crime of violence. Widom also determined that the arrestees in the study who self-reported a childhood of neglect were the most likely to commit a violent offense in adult life. Research conducted by Smith and Thornberry (1995) demonstrated that adolescents with histories of maltreatment at home self-reported violent behavior in adolescence.

Adult caregivers in the families of juvenile firesetters were identified as providing harsh and inconsistent discipline with absent or non-involved emotionally unavailable parents who demonstrated poor problem-solving and communication skills (Kelso & Stewart, 1986; Kolko & Kazdin, 1991). An interesting study produced by Sakheim and Osborn in 1986 compared twenty juvenile firesetters with a control group of non-firesetters. They concluded that the youth who experienced severe rejection by their families or were abandoned, abused or emotionally deprived of nurturance were more likely to be firesetters. The text will further explore the relationship between firesetting behavior and family life in succeeding chapters.

Age of Onset

The age of onset for firesetting behavior has received relatively little research attention and the focus has been primarily on male firesetters. In an article on female firesetters, Gold (1962) states that, in her experience, female firesetters range in age from five to eighty-four. The Wall Street Journal in an article published in June, 2003 cites a number of sources that discuss the age of childhood firesetters, at the time the behavior is recognized.

The article indicates that 41 percent of firesetters are identified between ages eight and twelve, 9 percent under age seven and 49 percent between ages thirteen and eighteen. Review of the literature on firesetting, reveals that opinions about age of onset vary depending, in large part, on the researcher's own experiences and understanding of the behavior. Fineman (1980) stated that most fires are set by curious boys between ages five and ten. Jacobson (1985) stated that firesetting peaks at age eight in conduct disordered boys while a study by Cox-Jones, Lubetsky, Fultz, and Kolko (1990) determined that firesetting occurred in two age clusters: around age eight and age thirteen. The Center for Arson Research posits that age of onset depends on the motivation for firesetting and assists in the determination of the specific subtype. Age of onset is described comprehensively in the following chapters on arson subtypes.

Common Diagnoses

Heath et al. (1985) reviewed the files of 204 youth seen in an outpatient clinic and determined a strong link between firesetting and the diagnosis of conduct disorder. Jacobson (1985) stated that firesetters comprised a subgroup of juveniles who had severe early age conduct disordered behavior. This group was characterized by more severely aggressive and antisocial conduct than their non-firesetting peers. According to studies conducted by Showers and Pickrell, (1987) and Kolko and Kadzin, (1991), juvenile firesetters were determined to be more aggressive and antisocial than their non-firesetter counter parts diagnosed with conduct disorder. However, research by Hanson et al. (1994) found no differences between youth diagnosed with conduct disorder other than the firesetting behavior itself. On the other hand, in the little research available on female firesetters, Stewart (1993) found that 92 percent of female arsonists carried a psychiatric diagnosis, generally depression. The lack of universality in understanding motivation, along with the small samples found in many studies of youth and adults, have contributed to gaps of knowledge and areas of disagreement in diagnosis. Williams (1999) mentions that many conclusions about juvenile firesetters are based on research into adult arsonists. Vreeland and Waller (1979) note that the problems of understanding classification and motivation of firesetters inhibit confidence into scientific research of the behavior.

Chapter 2

The Experimental or Curiosity Firesetter

Siddy, age four, and his little brother, Carl, age three, got up very early one morning and went downstairs. They were very quiet and did not awaken their mother. Siddy found a pack of matches on the dining room table and showed them to Carl who said, "You're gonna' get in trouble for touching them; they're bad!" Both boys giggled at the prospect of such rule-breaking behavior and Siddy suggested that they play a game of super heroes and "make an explosion in a cave." They excitedly gathered newspapers and, carrying them and the pack of matches, returned to their bedroom. Siddy and Carl crumpled newspapers and put them on the floor in their closet and arranged "bad guys" around the paper; Siddy stuck several matches to the paper and as it ignited, both boys watched the flames shoot upwards toward their clothes. Getting scared, they closed the closet door and ran back downstairs to the kitchen. Fortunately, their mother heard them running and smelled smoke, averting what might have been a tragedy. The brothers had never "played with matches" before this incident and had never showed any untoward interest in fire.

Curiosity and experimentation are normal parts of the childhood experience. Until fairly recently in our history, children were viewed as small adults, capable of logical and rational thought. The ways they reasoned were believed to be the same ways that adults thought and children were held equally accountable as adults for errors in judgment and conduct. Rousseau, an eighteenth century French philosopher, proposed that children reasoned differently than adults, qualitatively and quantitatively. Rousseau posited that children began to explore the world around them at birth, adding to their knowledge in an orderly progression of experiences and information. Early theories on what constituted childhood were

17

largely speculative and had little basis in scientific study. The emergence of psychology in the nineteenth century created an understanding of the value of direct observation and children began to be studied as a group by various social researchers, such as Watson and Gesell (Wilson & Kneisl, 1983).

In the 1950s, Jean Piaget studied children to determine the relationship between environmental influences and genetic attributes on cognitive development in childhood. He determined that children gained knowledge as they matured and they replaced earlier ideas and concepts with increasingly more complex ideas. He felt that each phase of cognitive development based itself on the previous phase and served as the foundation for the next phase. Piaget determined that the goal of development was to produce a person who could think logically and reason abstractly. Through painstaking observations of his own three children and others, Piaget (1958) developed complex theories about how young children develop cognitive skills to master the world around them. One of the valuable lessons gleaned from Piaget's seminal research into cognitive development was that children do think differently from adults.

Other theories have emerged since Piaget's initial work with children that focused primarily on cognitive development and largely ignored emotional and personality growth. Freud proposed that children develop through psychosexual stages that focus on body zones and that maturation determines when the shift from one body zone to another will occur (Freud, 1946). Abraham Maslow (1954) posited that humans are able to develop cognitively and emotionally only when basic needs, such as shelter and food, are met. Geneticist researchers, such as Plomin and Rende (1991) believe that environmental influences are as important as genetics in the development of the human potential.

Understanding cognitive development in children is of enormous importance in recognizing the dynamics that would cause little boys like Siddy and his younger brother to set a fire. According to Piaget (1954), children are at a preoperational stage of cognitive development from about age three to about age seven. During this phase of cognitive growth, children think in symbols but without logic although they are capable of reflecting on their actions. Children at the preoperational stage confuse reality and fantasy and have little ability to recognize the consequences of their actions. They are not able to think simultaneously about several aspects of a situation, focusing instead on only one component, something that often causes children to arrive at faulty conclusions (Papalia & Olds, 1995).

That lack of logical understanding about behavioral consequences helps to explain why some young children set fires in the preoperational stage of cognitive development. Andrew Muckley, a psychologist in the United Kingdom who works intensively with early childhood firesetters, believes that curiosity about fire is natural, especially since most children do not grow up in homes where fire is used as a source of heat (Muckley, 1997). He notes that fire is a natural phenomenon and that most children of today only encounter it when birthday candles are lit or someone lights a cigarette. The natural curiosity of young children may lead them to perceive of matches and lighter as toys within such a limited context. That curiosity can lead to a young child setting a fire with serious and unintended consequences.

The Center for Arson Research generally refers curiosity or experimental firesetters to fire safety and intervention programs. We use the term "curiosity or experimental" for this subtype interchangeably to indicate that the firesetter did not intend to cause harm or damage from malice. Of the 310 subjects in the study, only five (2 percent) were determined to be curiosity or experimental firesetters. It is our experience that this subtype is opportunistic and spontaneous in its firesetting behavior. Children who fit into this subtype are generally quite young, seven and under, who find matches or a lighter, and in the absence of adult supervision for that moment in time, set a fire. Youthful curiosity firesetters have a number of characteristics related to their firesetting behavior that are unique to that subtype. The few subjects in our random sample of 310 firesetters shared the following characteristics: with the exception of a three-year-old (the youngest subject in the sample), the remaining four set one fire each; the three-year-old set two fires. The mean age of the subtype was 6.5 years; one subject was white and the remaining four were African American. All five set their fires between the ages of three to ten years.

Comparison of this subtype with all other subtypes revealed some interesting, but inconclusive, findings due to the small sample. None of the following factors listed in Table 2.1 are found in the curiosity/experimental subtype.

Table 2.1
Comparisons Between the Experimental and All Other Subtypes

Variable	Experimental Subtype	All Other Subtypes
Rapid Mood Swings	0%	36%
Cruelty to Animals	0%	15%
Cruelty to Children	0%	18%
Property Destruction	0%	60%
Easily Led	0%	43%
Thrill Seeking	0%	13%
Homicidal Thoughts/Plans	0%	8%
Family Criminal Justice History	0%	8%
Revenge History	0%	17%
Fires Planned	0%	17%
Accelerants Used	0%	23%
Bomb-Making Knowledge	0%	7%
Mental Health History	0%	40%

A review of other variables revealed information also of interest but still inconclusive due to the small sample size. No conclusions should be drawn from the results while, at the same time, a number of the findings point to the need for additional study. The reader is reminded that behavioral histories are drawn from first person interviews and supportive documentation. Consideration of the findings suggest a need for further study that would help to explain why this group, overall, sets only one fire while sharing a similar history in certain of the variables (see Table 2.1). At the time of the interviews for the experimental subtypes, one of the subjects was seventeen years old and the other was forty-six years old. Although both subjects clearly recalled one time incidents of firesetting in early childhood (substantiated in their records), neither of them had set any more fires, although both were involved in ongoing asocial behavior. One subject reported involvement with the justice system in adolescence and both reported substance abuse histories. None of the five subjects was able to recall any specific feeling state before or during the act of firesetting and no one could explain where the idea to set a fire originated.

Table 2.2
Additional Comparisons Between Experimental and
All Other Subtypes

Variable	Experimental Subtype	All Other Subtypes
Special Education	60%	26%
Family Discord	80%	76%
Impulsive Behavior	60%	86%
Absent Parent(s)	80%	68%
Substance Abues by Parent(s)	60%	38%
Substance Abuse by Self	40%	80%
History of Abuse	60%	50%
Suicidal Thoughts/Attempts	40%	31%
Juvenile Justice History	20%	36%
Set Fire(s) Alone	80%	43%
Intervention Attempt	20%	29%
Remorse for Behavior	20%	26%

Each subject presented the fire event as a spontaneous act, unrelated to anything other than opportunity.

Curiosity/experimental firesetters demonstrate a number of characteristics that suggest additional areas of research. One key area, again recognizing the small number of subjects in this sample, is that despite the positive findings of variables in Table 2.1, firesetting did not continue as a behavior of choice. The writer notes that those variables are found, to a greater or lesser degree, in the other subtypes who report firesetting behavior that continues over time. There seems to be other factors that influence the decision not to set additional fires by the curiosity/ experimental subtype. At first blush, the reader will find that a key difference may lie with the motivation leading to firesetting behavior and the perception of the act itself (see Tables 2.1 and 2.2). A review of variables in the other subtypes, along with anecdotal information, may provide some understanding about the ways in which firesetters think about their fires. Cognitive development theory proposes that the way people organize their thinking about rules and laws influences them to be law-abiding citizens or criminals. Piaget (discussed earlier in this chapter) believed that there are two stages in the development of cognitive rule organization leading to socially responsible behavior. The first stage develops between ages ten to thirteen when the belief is that rules and laws are unchangeable and divine and a second stage, starting around age thirteen, when rules and laws are recognized as designed by people and therefore are fallible (Piaget, 1932).

Lawrence Kohlberg, a psychologist considered the founder of moral development theory, modified Piaget's theory and determined that moral reasoning developed in three phases divided into six distinct stages (see Table 2.3).

The first phase, found in stages one and two, Kohlberg called preconventional morality and he applied it to children between ages four to ten. In this phase, children are under external controls and obey rules to

Table 2.3
Kohlberg's Stages of Development

Stage	Moral Reasoning
Stage I	Right is obedience to power and avoidance of punishment.
Stage II	Right is taking responsibility for oneself, meeting one's own needs, and assuming no responsibility for others.
Stage III	Right means having good motives, having concern for others, and "putting yourself in another person's shoes".
Stage IV	Right is maintaining the rules of society and serving the welfare of the group or society.
Stage V	Right is based on individual rights within a society with agreed upon rules.
Stage VI	Right is an assumed obligation to principles to al: justice, equality, and respect for human life.

avoid punishment and gain rewards. The second phase, called conventional morality, is found in stages three and four. Children at this level of moral reasoning are between the ages of ten to thirteen and want to please others by being considered good boys and girls by those whose opinions matter to them. At this phase of development, standards of moral behavior are internalized and rules are followed because they are "right". The third phase, postconventional morality, starts sometime after age thirteen and involves doing the right thing in society because it is morally correct to do so. At this stage, the individual recognizes that there can be conflict around socially acceptable standards. Control of behavior is internalized and the person thinks for himself or herself to solve moral dilemmas. This level of moral thought, based upon personal beliefs about justice, human rights and duty does not really begin, according to Kohlberg, until after the age of twenty.

Kohlberg (1969) studied seventy-five boys for over twenty years who were between the ages of ten to sixteen when his longitudinal study began. He related stories to them that presented challenges to moral issues and had justice as the central theme and asked them how they would resolve the moral dilemma present in each hypothetical tale. Papalia and Olds (1995) note that Kohlberg was less interested in the answers by the subjects than in the reasoning that took place for them to arrive at their conclusions. There are a number of valid criticisms about Kohlberg's research. One is that the subjects were all American boys, effectively precluding valid conclusions about the moral reasoning of girls or other cultural groups. Additionally, some other researchers, such as Carroll and Rest (1982) found that moral reasoning skills are developed through education, essentially by telling children what is a right course of action instead of expecting them to figure things out on their own. At the same time, it is clear that knowing the right course of an action does not necessarily guarantee that the correct choice will be made. However, moral reasoning theory, whatever its shortcomings, has added to our body of knowledge about how children learn socially and morally acceptable behavior.

The research by Kohlberg (1969) also added to our understanding of the development of moral learning and its association to cognitive development. When he applied his moral reasoning model to the study of criminals, Kohlberg and his associates (1973) determined that offenders had significantly lower moral judgment development than their non-criminal counterparts. He conjectured that criminals made decisions about right and wrong based on a different evaluation process than did non-criminals. In fact, while law-abiding citizens consider the reactions of their families and friends, criminals consider possible legal sanctions and do not consider the reactions of others to their behavior. Additionally, while the average citizen regards rules and laws as beneficial to society, criminals tend to view them only within the narrow context of their self-interest.

Summary

The small sample size of five curiosity/experimental firesetters prohibits an in-depth understanding of the behavior but presents an opportunity for further study. Although the histories of the five subjects reflect similar findings in the other subtypes, the group of curiosity/ experimental firesetters is distinctive for their discontinued firesetting behavior while continuing to demonstrate other socially unacceptable behavior. Consideration of Kohlberg's Moral Reasoning Theory suggests the possibility that the fear of sanctions for the behavior might have been an instrumental cause but does not explain why this sample responded to sanctions for firesetting behavior while the other subtypes generally do not. Of interest is the finding that no one of the subjects received intervention other than the strong disapproval of adults in their lives. Additional research into differences and similarities in the subtypes will advance understanding of positive approaches to interrupt firesetting behavior in young children. The Center for Arson Research recognizes that firesetting in young children is often opportunistic and reflects no more than the lack of reasoning and good judgment associated with the very young.

Chapter 3

The Delinquent Firesetter

Kerry is a fourteen-year-old adolescent who has been in a lot of trouble over the past year. He is on probation for breaking into two vending machines and vandalizing school property. He refuses to listen to his mother who has been a single parent for the last four years. Kerry estimates that he has been in "About fifty fights at school; I don't start them; I stop them." He has been shoplifting things from local stores. "I'm good at it and security guards are all wack, anyway." He is failing ninth grade and has had multiple suspensions for repeated truancy, disrespectful language, and conflicts with his teachers. Kerry hangs around with a group of older youth who encourage his negative behavior. He smokes marijuana daily and drinks beer whenever it is available. Last week, he was arrested with three other boys for breaking into a home under construction, which they vandalized by ripping the plumbing fixtures from the walls and breaking all the windows. The leader of the group ordered Kerry to set a fire in the living room area to "get rid of the evidence". The resultant arson caused $300,000.00 worth of damage.

The concept of delinquency is a relatively new cultural idea that determined that criminal acts committed by youthful offenders should be weighed differently than those same acts if committed by an adult. Before the nineteenth century, children were treated in the same way as adults by authorities with an emphasis on severe punishment for disobedience. The philosophy to view children and youth separately from adults under the law arose by the end of the 1800s, as a group of progressive social reformers identified factors they believed contributed to deviant behavior in the young. The United States was undergoing rapid industrialization and urbanization that, at that time, combined with the influx of a huge immigrant population to create an underclass identified by some reformers as

25

having the potential towards deviant behavior. Children were regarded by their parents and business owners as cheap labor sources and many immigrant children went to work at young ages for very long hours resulting in minimal education and little actual contact with their families. Members of the Progressive Movement who called themselves the child savers decided it was their duty to rescue and rehabilitate these immigrant children from the potential dangers of poverty and the possible deviant influences of their families (Gaines, Kuane, & Miller, 2001).

The child savers were instrumental in influencing various state legislatures to pass laws that permitted them to take custody of (generally) immigrant children who were suffering from perceived parental neglect or youth who showed signs of criminal behavior. According to Schmalleger (1997), New York City and other industrialized cities of the northeast responded to the assumed needs of these children by developing "houses of refuge" where youth, forcibly removed from their homes, were placed. The children sent to these institutions were most often thieves, vagrants, and runaways. There they received rehabilitation in the form of hard labor, a popular method of reform in the mid-nineteenth century. The concept of physical labor was based around a Christian principle that idleness was an invitation to trouble and that work was essential for feelings of self-worth. Youth who were more seriously delinquent went to prisons where they were confined with adult criminals as did other youth when houses of refuge were too crowded.

By the mid-nineteenth century, another approach embraced by the child savers was the reform school, initially modeled after a traditional Christian home. The child savers envisioned reform schools as places to send youth who demonstrated delinquent tendencies before they became actual criminals. In such environments, children were supposed to receive those values and morals that would enable them to lead good Christian lives and eschew delinquency (Schmalleger, 1997). Widespread efforts directed at reforming pre-delinquent youth soon led to problems with overcrowding, as in the original houses of refuge and the vision of reformation was replaced by institutionalization.

Finally, through the efforts of the child savers, the Illinois Juvenile Court Act passed in 1899 and established the first court specifically to consider cases involving youth. The system was based on the doctrine of parens patriae, a philosophy which held the state to have a duty to be responsible for children who were neglected, delinquent or disadvantaged. The principle posited that adults, acting on behalf of the state, recognized that children were not fully responsible for their criminal conduct and that they were capable of full rehabilitation (Inciardi, 1997).

Juvenile courts differed significantly from adult court in a number of significant ways when the concept was established and many of those reforms still exist today. Judges decided issues without the presence of a jury and with the focus on the youth, not the crime. Petitions rather than warrants were issued, and juveniles were found "adjudicated delinquent", not "guilty." There was no adversarial relationship between the court and the youth and all parties gathered to determine what was best for the juvenile as they considered rehabilitation. Finally, all court hearings were confidential and closed to the public in order to protect the youth from the stigma of criminal behavior (Gaines, Kaune & Miller, 2001).

Delinquency is defined as a criminal law violation that would be considered a crime if committed by an adult (Inciardi, 1997). In considering the problems of juveniles, the state, through juvenile court, has responsibility for oversight and intervention in those cases where youth do not, or could not, benefit from the guidance and care of their parents. Juvenile court also holds responsibility for attempts at intervention for behaviors such as truancy and curfew violation. Those violations, called status offenses, describe behavior considered illegal if performed by a person below a certain age (Inciardi, 1997). Status offenses are often considered pre-delinquent behaviors that, if uninterrupted, segue into delinquency. The movement towards decriminalizing status offenses arose through the 1960s into the 1970s as recognition that treating runaways and other status offenders as delinquents exposed many minors to hard-core youthful criminals in reform schools and prisons. Inciardi points out that the volume of status offenders is over-whelming with approximately 40 percent of juveniles appearing in juvenile court for a status violation. Much of the available resources of juvenile court systems are taken up with status offenses rather than in addressing the more serious issue of juvenile crime and criminals.

Social Disorganization Theory

Social science researchers have long attempted to explain delinquent behavior. One of the earliest explanations proposed was by Clifford Shaw and Henry McKay, based upon research they conducted in the 1920s and

30s. Social disorganization theory (also known as social ecology) was conceptualized at the University of Chicago as a way to study urban crime and delinquency. Shaw and McKay plotted out the homes of delinquents referred to juvenile court in Chicago and developed a number of interesting findings. They determined that the rates of delinquency were highest towards the inner city and decreased towards areas of affluence. Additionally, Shaw and McKay (1969) found that the rates of delinquency remained constant, despite population turnover and changes in ethnicity and race in the inner city.

Using an earlier theory of plant and animal ecology, Shaw and McKay posited that a city reflected the natural community with specific zones that radiated from a central core to outside, concentric rings. They believed that the center core of a city was the business and commercial zone and that the next concentric ring reflected transitional living. This transitional zone represented the highest degree of delinquency and held a number of distinct characteristics. Newly arrived immigrants and many poor, uneducated people moving up from the south were attracted to transitional zone neighborhoods because of their ability to find cheap housing, albeit in deplorable condition. There were few homeowners but many transient renters without links to the community. Residents often had very little in common with one another except poverty and unemployment. Places of residence were not physically maintained and the residents had little upward mobility potential. Transitional zones also had high crime rates, prostitution, drug abuse, alcoholism, domestic violence, and mental illness. Analyzing data for a sixty-five-year span, Shaw and McKay (1942) found that the inner city zones remained consistent with high crime and delinquency rates, despite changes in ethnic composition.

Shaw and McKay (1969) believed that delinquency was the result of the social disorganization found in the transitional zone. They argued that the lack of social order created a weakened social structure network unable to respond adequately to an unstable, heterogeneous population. The researchers posited that delinquency was a natural result of a community without social integration and with weakened social supports such as strong families, good schools, churches with positive ties to the neighborhood, and jobs. Shaw and McKay thought that delinquency and crime were normal responses to living conditions under abnormal circumstances.

Shaw and McKay (1942) believed that the community was responsible for supervision and control over teenagers and that the lack of ability in a community to control their youth led to delinquent conduct. As a result of the findings from their study, the first large-scale delinquency prevention program in the United States was launched in Chicago. Called the Chicago Area Project, self-help centers that were staffed by community volunteers, opened in a number of high delinquency, lower-class neighborhoods. Each center offered camps, educational opportunities, counseling, recreation, and discussion groups. Results were mixed, but delinquency rates were reduced in a number of neighborhoods and Shaw and McKay (1969) were reinforced in their belief that social organization could reduce crime and delinquency.

Social disorganization gained currency following the successes of the Chicago Area Project, but it remains unclear as to the extent that a disorganized society can explain the presence of crime. One problem mentioned by Akers (1997) is that social ecology research does not carefully measure social disorganization. In fact, Akers points out the circular reasoning inherent in studies on inner city crime by noting that the fact that if crime is high in an area, that finding is used as an indicator that it is disorganized. He also notes that even those areas of great disorganization have small numbers of residents, adult and juvenile, actually committing crimes. Social disorganization theory holds that residents of an impoverished neighborhood have little investment in their community and want only to get out. This desire to flee weakens social institutions, such as the family, and peer groups (gangs) replace the family as centers of influence, creating delinquency.

Wilson (1987) observed that a trend for both white and black middle class residents of all ethnicities was the move from the city to the suburbs. This migration away from city life also included the migration of businesses and industry, leaving the inner cities facing greater social deprivation. Wilson noted that the residents left in the inner cities were the truly disadvantaged who suffer from helplessness, hopelessness, poverty, addiction, and despair. Akers (1997) stated that arrests, convictions, and other measures of crime continue to be high in inner city neighborhoods although the association between social disorganization and crime remains unclear.

Strain Theory

There are, of course, other theories about the causes of crime and delinquency; this chapter addresses a number of them relevant to the discussion of delinquent firesetting behavior. The reader should be aware that the theories under discussion are by no means exhaustive, but are meant to be reflective of areas of theoretical study on delinquency. It is important for any student of crime to note that most of the research into crime and delinquency causation focuses on urban residents and that relatively little study is conducted on suburban and rural children and youth and their families. Strain theory, for example, proposes that crime is the direct result of frustration and anger experienced by inner-city poor who feel ostracized by society. Strain theorists propose that most people share middle-class values largely unattainable by the lower class. This inability to attain those goals produces emotional and economic strain which results in some individuals deciding to turn to crime as a way to reach their goals and others to reject middle class values and turn to deviant goals instead. Siegel (2004) traces the roots of strain theory back to Èmile Durkheim's theory of anomie, founded in his study of the causes of suicide. Durkheim, a well-known French sociologist, believed that a society undergoing some period of transition, either man-made or because of a natural disaster, suffered from social turmoil that disconnected people from one another, causing a feeling of strain. This sense of disconnection, or anomie, created a vacuum where social control once existed and the community no longer shared the common goal of social order.

Robert Merton, an American sociologist, revised Durkheim's theory of anomie in 1938 to fit modern American society. Merton (1968) suggested that all social and cultural structures are characterized by the elements of goals (what people want) and means (socially approved methods of achieving goals). The norms of our society define the methods we may use to obtain our culturally sanctioned goals. In American society, our main goals are centered around the acquisition of money, power, and success. According to Merton, legitimate means of obtaining those goals are divided along class lines. The poor and under-educated are denied most socially-acceptable means to achieve their ambitions and may develop criminal or delinquent behaviors to reach desired goals.

According to Merton (1968), each person has his or her own methods for adapting to the goals of society. He identified five specific modes of adaptation commonly used by those responding to goals and means. The first, *conformity*, is acceptance of society's goals and the methods for achieving them and is the most commonly used and socially sanctioned adaptive method of reaching goals. The second mode of adaptation is *innovation*, the acceptance of society's goals but rejection of, or inability to use, the legitimate means of reaching them. The third mode is *ritualism*, which is rejection of socially sanctioned goals but acceptance of the means. Reid (1997) observes that ritualism involves people doing something they "should", such as attending a church, even if the experience has no meaning to them.

The fourth mode of adaptation, *retreatism*, signals a complete rejection of both the goals and means of society. Reid mentions that retreatism is the least common of the five adaptive styles occurring after an individual has tried and repeatedly failed to achieve goals through socially-sanctioned means. Such an individual, for whatever reason, cannot attempt to achieve goals through illegal means and so he or she withdraws from society, defeated. The final mode, *rebellion*, signals the rejection of socially acceptable means and goals with alternative ones that reflect an attempt to change the social order.

Although Merton's model has received popular support since its publication, Merton, himself, had criticisms of his theory. He noted it does not explain why or how an individual selects one mode of adaptation over another. Anomic theory does not explore rebellion thoroughly and does not identify the elements of an individual's social structure that may be influential on behavior (Merton, 1968). Other critics of strain theory propose that Merton fails to explain why people choose certain crimes over others or why many youth grow up and out of delinquency. Additionally, strain theory seems rather shortsighted about the nature of adolescence itself. Teenagers tend to live in the "here and now" with goals related to their immediate future, not long-term achievements. Strain theory suggests that all people share the same goals and expectations; in fact, individuals may vary widely about their measures of success (Messner & Rosenfeld, 1994).

The Center for Arson Research identified 115 delinquents (37 percent) of the total 310 firesetting subjects randomly selected for this textbook. Although the Center for Arson Research does not collect data on the social class status of its clients, approximately 75 percent of the delinquent youth evaluated arose from a lower socioeconomic group. Note: This approximate finding is based on data collected elsewhere and reviewed by the writer. The finding that the majority of referrals in this subtype were from a lower socioeconomic status may be reflective that youth from lower class families are less protected from the juvenile justice system and may be more likely to face intervention and placement than youth from middle and upper class families. Firesetters are characterized in the literature as of a lower socioeconomic status (Heath et al., 1985, Showers & Pickrell, 1987) although studies by Kosky & Silburn (1984) and Kuhnley et al. (1982) failed to support that hypothesis.

Of interest is that half of the delinquent youth in the study appear to share the concept of dreams for their futures despite their class status, family backgrounds, opportunities, and abilities. While this finding is worth mentioning, it does seem that those individuals living in poverty and despair may be at a greater risk for criminal conduct, supporting the concept of strain and the impact of blocked goal attainment on behavior (Menard, 1995). The point is made, however, that although over 30 million Americans live below the poverty line, most individuals living in economic despair do not become criminals (Siegal, 2004). Table 3.1 demonstrates general demographics of the delinquent firesetter subtype in the study; the mean age of the subjects at the onset of their firesetting behavior was 13.6 years. The subjects were predominately male (94 percent), reinforcing the findings in the literature that firesetting is a male-dominated behavior (Gruber, Heck & Mintzer, 1981; Kolko, 1985; Bourget & Bradford, 1989; Siegel, 2003).

While it is clear that social class alone should not be used as an explanation of crime and delinquency, it must be considered along with other variables that seem related. Juvenile delinquency has traditionally been associated with the "broken home" concept, although current thinking points to conflict in the home as more significant than a single-parent family (Rosen & Neilson, 1982). Women are often head-of-household single parents who must contend with economic despair and have little choice in affordable housing. Children raised in high-crime areas may fall

Table 3.1
General Demographics of the 115 Delinquent Firesetters in the Center for Arson Research Study

Gender		
Female: 7 (0.6%)		Male: 108 (94%)
Race		
African-American: 55 (48%)	White: 52 (45%)	Other: 8 (7.0%)

under the influence of their community exposure to the delinquents and criminals around them (Felson & Cohen, 1980). In fact, studies by Loeber and Stouthamer-Loeber (1986) point to parental rejection as the most powerful predictor of delinquency. Clifford Shaw and Henry McKay, two social science researchers, were among the first to determine that broken homes were not necessarily a primary factor in delinquency (1931). Indeed, Shaw and McKay (1929) believed that delinquency was a result of social disorganization, characterized by economic instability and weakened social controls. More recent studies demonstrate that youth who grow up in homes where there is tension and conflict and without the benefit of a healthy intact family system appear at higher risk for delinquent behavior than do children in one-parent households (Siegel, 2003). The U.S. Census Bureau estimates that the number of children living in a two-parent household will fall to 29 percent by 2010. Of note is that of the 115 delinquent firesetters in the Center for Arson Research study, only 23 percent (twenty-seven clients) reported one or both of their parents absent from the home compared to 44 percent of the total population of firesetters in the study.

Social Process Theory

Social process theories, also called social learning theories, posit that delinquent and criminal behaviors are functions of the socialization of the individual and that people learn to behave in a law-abiding way or not, according to their interactions with others. Akers (1997) observed that the basic framework for social learning theory was developed by Edwin Sutherland, an extremely influential criminologist of the twentieth century.

Sutherland (1947) proposed that criminal behavior was either modeled or encouraged by friends and others with a meaningful relationship to the individual. He called this concept differential association and developed nine elements to his theory that explained how criminal behavior originates and is reinforced. The elements of differential association theory are:

- Criminal behavior is learned.
- Criminal behavior is learned through interaction with others.
- The principal part of learning criminal behavior occurs in small intimate groups.
- Learning includes crime techniques (the "how-to" of criminal activity) as well. as the imposition of motives, attitudes, drives, and rationalizations.
- The specific direction of drives and motives is learned from definitions of the legal code as favorable or unfavorable.
- A person becomes delinquent because there are more favorable than unfavorable definitions to violation of law.
- Differential associations may vary in frequency, duration, priority, and intensity. This point is crucial to Sutherland's theory as it implies that if an individual is exposed initially and with more frequency over a longer period of time and attaches great importance to those interactions, he or she is more likely to be delinquent (Akers, 1997).
- The processes for learning criminal behavior are the same processes used to learn anything else.
- Criminal behavior is an expression of general needs and values, but that does not explain criminal conduct because non-criminal behavior also expresses general needs and values.

There were criticisms to the theory of differential association, among them the observation that people can embrace criminal behavior without ever actually meeting a criminal, while another was that it was too ambiguous to be really meaningful. Cressey (1970), writing in defense of differential association, said that the theory proposed that individuals became criminals not because of exposure to criminals per se, but rather because of a concentrated exposure to criminal attitudes. Review of the data on the 115 delinquent firesetters in the Center for Arson Research study reveals that 42 percent of the group reported a juvenile justice history, excluding firesetting, in comparison to 36 percent of the overall population of firesetters in all other subtypes, while 54 percent claimed to set fires while in the company of peers. It is fair to note that many of the fires set by delinquents occurred to cover up the commission of another crime or as an act of vandalism or property destruction, according to their arrest records.

Positive family relationships seem to be pivotal in delinquency prevention. Specific factors, such as poor or inconsistent parental discipline, marital discord, abuse, neglect, and parent criminality all contribute to negative behavior in children and youth. Quality of life in the home of delinquents appears to have more disruption than in the homes of non-delinquents (Sakheim & Osborn, 1986; Kelso & Stewart, 1986). The delinquent firesetters in the Center for Arson Research study self-report family discord in 70 percent of the interviews in comparison to the total population of all other firesetters at 79 percent. In another variable, absent parent, found in Table 3.2, delinquent firesetters in the sample report having both parents present in their lives and homes in a significant departure from the self-reports of the other firesetter respondents. As a cohort, delinquent firesetters also report less abuse overall as well as fewer suicide attempts and little solitary firesetting, in comparison to all other subtypes.

Social Control Theory

Travis Hirschi (1969) developed social control theory as an attempt to explain the elements that create law-abiding behavior in youth. He determined that adolescents who have little regard for or conformity to social mores are a greater risk for delinquent conduct. Hirschi proposed that a common value system and social bond created the desire to conform to acceptable and lawful conduct in our society. This social bond, according to Hirschi, has four components: *involvement* with conventional others, *belief* in conventional social norms, *attachment* to conventional people, and *commitment* to conventional behavior. Hirschi believed that weakened elements of the social bond increased the likelihood of delinquent behavior.

To test his hypothesis, Hirschi (1969) collected data from self-report questionnaires completed by slightly over 4,000 California junior and senior high school students. The respondents were asked about their attitudes towards family, friends, and community along with their attitudes

Table 3.2
**Comparing Delinquent Firesetters and Other Subtypes
in Certain Variables**

Variable	Delinquent Subtype	All Other Subtypes
Special Education	23%	28%
Family Discord	79%	70%
Impulsive Behavior	81%	89%
Absent Parent	23%	68%
Substance-Use Parent	33%	41%
Substance-Use Self	23%	33%
Physical Abuse History	21%	31%
Sexual Abuse History	4%	13%
Emotional Abuse History	10%	19%
All Three (Types of Abuse)	1%	0.05%
Suicidal Attempts	12%	23%
Juvenile Justice History	42%	32%
Set Fire(s) Alone	16%	59%
Intervention Attempt	17%	21%
Remorse for Behavior	27%	23%

about parents, teachers, and school. Additionally, they answered six questions about delinquent behavior, indicating whether (1) they never committed the offense, (2) committed the offense more than a year ago, (3) committed the offense during the past year, or (4) committed the offense during the past year and also more than a year ago.

Results of the study have proven to be of long-standing interest and social control theory has undergone rigorous empirical testing by many others over time. Hirschi made a number of significant contributions to the understanding of delinquency, among them:

- Findings did not support earlier studies linking socioeconomic class and delinquency. Hirschi found little to support the hypothesis that joined lower-class youth to delinquency. He noted, however, that boys in families where the father was unemployed or the family was on welfare were more likely than boys where the family was not on welfare and where there was gainful employment to engage in delinquent behavior.

- Boys with middle-class values are relatively unaffected by the delinquent behavior of their friends.
- Youth with little investment in conformity are susceptible to pre-delinquent influences.

Social control theory, although among the most influential and far-reaching of the theoretical models on delinquency (Bohm & Haley, 1973), is not without criticism. Siegel & Senna (1981) observe that social control theory does not explain how the social bond is initially broken and whether weakening in any element of the bond weakens the other elements. Additionally, Hirschi (1969) did not indicate whether a weak social bond could be strengthened or why most delinquents do not grow up to become criminals. A major shortcoming of social control theory is its contention that delinquents are friendless loners with little affection for others (Hirschi, 1969; Vandersall & Wiener, 1970; Vreeland & Levin, 1980). However, Giordano, Cernkovich & Pugh (1986) found that the friendships of delinquents resemble the relationships non-delinquents have with their peers. Sixty-seven percent of the delinquent subjects in the Center for Arson Research study report friendships with others. In fact, during interviews, delinquent firesetters tend to characterize themselves as very popular with peers and overwhelmingly report that they have "always had lots of friends".

Containment Theory

Criminologic theories, in general, attempt to explain crime causation. Some theorists, such as Travis Hirschi and Walter Reckless, focused less on causation and more on social constraints in their work on delinquent boys. Reckless (1961) argued that youth resisted crime based upon certain forces that he called inner and outer containments. Inner containments are factors such as a social conscience, a positive self-image and the ability to withstand frustration. Outer containments relate to social roles and expectations, including elements such as good mentoring by parents and teachers and consistent moral teaching (Akers, 1997). According to Reckless' containment theory, some youth can avoid inducements to behave in a delinquent manner because they possess outer and inner strengths that allow them to avoid the pitfalls of negative conduct. Reckless believed that society offered youth various "pushes and pulls" towards delinquent behavior. Pushes are social conditions such as poverty and deprivation and pulls are delinquent peers or a delinquent subculture.

Reckless (1967) posited that youth who held positive self-images and had good self-esteem were insulated from the negative pushes and pulls of society and therefore were able to resist delinquent temptations. Kaplan (1980) believed that youth with a poor self-image are the group most likely to engage in delinquent behavior in order to raise their self-worth. Those youth find peers with similar compromised self-worth and together they engage in delinquent activities in order to experience unconventional success through criminal enterprise. It is tempting to wonder why, if poor self-regard influences youth to engage in socially-deviant behavior, many delinquents grow up and out of delinquency as they reach adulthood, even though their basic self-views and life experiences did not change. Of great research interest to us is our recognition that delinquent firesetters do not grow up, generally speaking, to become adult arsonists. As youth grow up, either out of delinquency or into adult criminality, they seem to abandon firesetting. It is not an infrequent experience for us to re-interview former clients who, in adulthood, have broken the law and because of a past history of firesetting, are evaluated pre-sentencing or placement. Despite continued criminal conduct, most former delinquent firesetters leave setting fires behind them, perhaps because their law-breaking activities, in adult life, are not committed to impress others. For those youthful firesetters who grow up to be crime-free, a number of the variables as seen in Tables 3.2 and 3.3 may point to factors that aide, overall, in resisting the temptations of adult criminality. Factors such as friendships with others, a lack of revenge mind-set, an intact family system (even if in discord), and plans for the future provide a foundation that may be worthy of additional study. Certain variables that reflect attitudes, behaviors and life experiences and are commonly associated with delinquent conduct are listed in Table 3.3 for consideration.

An earlier study by Williams (1998), examined delinquent firesetting behavior in a small random sample of twenty youth between the ages of seven and sixteen years. The study examined possible motivations for setting fires in delinquents and another firesetting subtype, disordered coping, a group to be discussed in a succeeding chapter in this textbook. The

Table 3.3
Comparisons of Certain Behavioral Variables in Delinquent Firesetters and all Other Subtypes by Percentage

Variable	Delinquent Subtype	All Other Subtypes
Cruelty to Animals	8%	19%
Property Destruction	55%	63%
Easily Led	40%	44%
Thrill-Seeking	11%	14%
Excessive Anger	54%	73%
Family Criminal Justice History	6%	.08%
Juvenile Justice History	42%	32%
Revenge-Seeking	10%	21%
Mental Health History	31%	46%
Friendship with Peers	67%	42%
Learning Problems	47%	55%
Hyperactivity	50%	67%
Impulsivity	81%	89%

results of that earlier study are compared to the results from the larger study of 115 delinquent firesetters in Table 3.4. None of the earlier respondents are included in the larger study. Respondents had the opportunity to identify as many motivating factors as applicable in each of the studies. Respondents in both studies identified peer pressure as the primary motivator for firesetting behavior while a number of the subjects acknowledged feelings of anger or the need for revenge. A number of respondents in both groups either were unaware of their motives for setting fires or elected not to identify their motivation to the interviewer. The writer suggests that an examination of each subtype will produce statistical changes in the motivation variable.

Identifying the Delinquent Firesetter

Despite the fact that many resources are readily available on the identification, intervention and treatment of delinquency, relatively little is available on delinquent firesetters. In acknowledgement of the wealth of data available on the study of delinquency (and our own wide experience in the

Table 3.4
Motivations of Deliquent Firesetters in Two Studies

	Don't Know	Anger	Excitement	Peer Pressure	Revenge	Other
Delinquents (1998) 20 Subjects	15%	5%	20%	50%	10%	0%
Delinquents (2003) 115 Subjects	28%	5.2%	5.2%	47%	0%	12.8%

treatment of delinquents overall), we did not study "garden-variety" delinquents as an entity and elected not to use a control group of non-firesetting delinquents to replicate an already rich area of research. Firesetting in children and youth is generally regarded as delinquent behavior (no matter what the motive) and is considered as part of a conduct disorder, a common mental health diagnosis for juvenile firesetters (Heath et al. 1985). Twenty years worth of data collection on firesetting behavior has given us a unique opportunity to identify certain key variables found in the delinquent firesetter subtype that may or may not be present in delinquents without firesetting behavior. Our interest was in the observation that these factors are either not found in the other subtypes or are identified but to a significantly greater or lesser degree. One of the most interesting observations from our research has been the recognition that firesetting behavior in the delinquent subtype has its onset generally in early to mid-adolescence while other delinquent behavior begins during or before latency. In the sample of 115 delinquent firesetters, for example, the mean age for the onset of firesetting was thirteen years, six months, while the mean age for other delinquent behavior was eleven years, three months. Table 3.5 describes a number of variables that relate to delinquency and compares delinquent firesetters to other subtypes in the study. As the reader will note, differences in the subtypes are quite evident in the variables that relate to firesetting itself.

Note: Seven percent of delinquent firesetters deny all firesetting behavior despite arrests for the act. Five percent claim to have set "multiple" fires while 15 percent claim to have "no idea" of the number of fires they started.

Table 3.5
Comparisons of Variable Across Subtypes

	Delinquent	Revenge	Disordered Coping	Thrill-seeking	Psychotic
Property Destruction	55%	68%	68%	5%	55%
Fighting	57%	72%	71%	6%	82%
Theft	49%	60%	67%	6%	55%
Learning Problems	47%	57%	66%	6%	45%
Impulsive	81%	94%	90%	8%	91%
Chronic Lying	82%	87%	91%	8%	64%
Substance Abuse	23%	43%	22%	5%	73%
Remorse for Firesetting	27%	32%	20%	3%	37%
Fires Planned	9%	32%	17%	1%	45%
Average No. of Fires: <5 >5 >10	69% 2% 3%	62% 38% 0%	0% 79% 21%	0% 6% 3%	82% 18% 0%
Excessive Anger	54%	81%	76%	6%	64%
Age Firesetting Began (mean age)	13.6	10	6	7	18
Sets Fire Alone	16%	60%	66%	4%	64%
Accelerants Used	20%	32%	19%	1%	0%
Bomb Knowledge	0.02%	17%	3.0%	0%	18%
Attempts to Extinguish Fires or Warn Others	17%	23%	17%	2%	0%

Firesetting in an Adolescent Behavioral Context

It is a normal part of growth and development to break rules and conflict with adult authority figures. However, the youth in our study (and delinquents in general) develop behaviors that interfere with the development of socially appropriate conduct at home, in school, and in the community. The root causes of delinquency, as we have seen, are complex and reflect biological, social, familial, and environmental factors. Movement along the pathway into adult life means accommodating to vast changes in one's physical and psychological make-up. Most adolescents successfully bridge the distance between childhood and adult life with only some minor bumps along the development highway while others descend into asocial behavior, affecting self-esteem and producing frustration and anger.

Papalia and Olds (1995) point out that the central theme of adolescence is the search for one's own identity, a quest that lasts a lifetime. Erik Erikson (1950) indicated that the principal task of identity development is the ability to distinguish the self from others, especially one's parents. Erikson conceptualized adolescence as a time of experimentation with roles at home and with peers, undertaken to help youth define who they are. Traditionally, significant adults in the adolescents' lives are appointed, often unwillingly and unwittingly, as adversaries who must be resisted and rebelled against as an act of defiance against proscribed rules and values. Clashes between parent(s) and child are common in adolescence and Papalia and Olds observe that most conflicts are fairly minor and are worked out rather easily. However, when the youth is growing up in a household characterized by a high degree of discord as reported by 70 percent of the delinquent firesetters in the study, conflict resolution is neither quick nor easy.

There is, of course, variability in the ways and rates at which youth grow and mature. Steiner and Feldman (1996) in the text *Treating Adolescents*, discuss the developmental domains of adolescence: basic and bodily needs; interpersonal functioning; mental health functioning; academic and vocational functioning, and recreation and leisure functioning. They observe that basic and bodily functioning includes attention to one's health and hygiene, while interpersonal functioning relates to an ability to get along with parents and peers of both genders. Unell and Wyckoff (1995) note that the basis for establishing positive relationships with others is the development of the capacity to empathize; a virtue they believe that forms the foundation for all other social virtues. Surely we recognize the difference between an individual who has the capacity "to place himself in our shoes" versus one who has no clue. It is but a short walk from empathy to remorse for wrongdoing and our interactions with firesetters overall, indicate that they feel little remorse for wrongful behavior. Delinquent firesetters report experiencing remorse for their negative behavior (including firesetting) in 27 percent of the cases, while 23 percent of all other subtypes report feeling remorseful. Interestingly, 42 percent of the total population of all firesetters and 67 percent of the delinquents report having friendships with peers. We recommend that there is a need for further research interest in the concept of remorse and general delinquent behavior. On the face of our findings, a lack of remorse (and empathetic understanding) does not seem to prohibit delinquent firesetters from peer-related friendships. We will more closely examine friendships and remorse in succeeding chapters on other subtypes.

Steiner and Feldman (1996) describe mental health functioning as including self-esteem, insight into one's self, attachment, motivation, and affect/mood, while academic and vocational achievement includes planning for the future. Low self-esteem, in particular, has traditionally been identified in association with delinquency (Conger and Miller, 1966, and Rathus and Siegal, 1973). Doing poorly in school is considered contributory to lower self-esteem in youth (Gold, 1978). While 47 percent of the delinquent group report learning problems, 62 percent of all other subtypes acknowledge learning problems and both sets report problems with attention and concentration: delinquents (57 percent) and all others (62 percent).

In an interesting study conducted by Polk and Richmond (1978), students who did well in school had lower rates of delinquency than did youth who were viewed as low achievers or school failures by educational authorities. However, when they compared failure rates with social class, they determined that youth from middle- and upper-class families failed significantly less than youth from lower-class families. Polk and Shafer (1972) argued that the educational system contributed to the belief of low achievers that they could not succeed in the classroom, encouraging the students' sense of failure. As an anecdotal observation, many lower-income youth evaluated by the Center for Arson Research describe their dislike of school and believe they are "not good at it". The domain of positive academic and vocational functioning appears closed to many of the clients we have seen over the years.

The domain of leisure and recreational functioning is also problematic for delinquents in general. Youth involved in delinquent conduct often lack life goals and personal goals. Because they lack commitment to positives, it becomes easy for these adolescents and pre-teens to get into trouble. When we consider the 115 delinquent firesetters in our study (and we believe them to be a true representative sample of delinquent firesetters), we note that 81 percent of them self-report impulsive, thoughtless behavior as a problem in their lives. Impulsivity is also a problem in all other of the subtypes, as well at a reported 89 percent, but as we will discover in the other subtypes, their behavior appears more focused, purposeful and deliberate. Delinquent firesetters are easily bored and need stimulation and the excitement of wrongdoing, especially if it gains the admiration of their peer groups. We interview very few solitary delinquent firesetters. The impetus to set fires generally comes from a leader member of the peer group who directs the activities and escapades of the others. We differentiate here between a formal gang and a group; this study excludes those delinquents who are gang members.

Motivation

The idea of the fire is based upon either a desire to conceal some other crime, such as vandalism or burglary, or as a demonstration of what we call "gangster-light" behavior—done to impress others, without regard to possible consequences, victims, or a comprehension of the meaning of dollar loss. Delinquent firesetters do not have an emotional attachment to their fires, as such. Fire does not make them feel better, as it does for disordered coping firesetters, or satisfied, as it does for revenge setters. Unlike other subtypes, delinquent firesetters blame firesetting on peers and very few take personal responsibility for the idea, although they may admit the actual behavior.   Our experiences over the years have led us to conclude that loyalty to friends stops at the point of consequences for delinquent firesetters. One of the hallmarks in the assessment of a juvenile firesetter is his absolute willingness to implicate others and his denial of "being the guy with the idea" to set a fire. Interestingly enough, this shy reluctance to admit responsibility for a act of arson does not extend to other crimes, as we hear proud boasts of non-firesetting acts of delinquency from the very youth who deny the idea of firesetting during their interviews.

Prevention/Intervention Strategies and Gaps in Knowledge in Delinquent Firesetting Behavior

There is always a danger in relying solely on data collected from official sources, such as arrest records, because information can be skewed or eliminated, and official reports are incident-based, not person-oriented (Reiss & Roth, 1993). Motivation, chronicity of the offender, and personal history are missing from official data sources. Unfortunately, policy decisions about the scope of a problem (such as firesetting) along with possible intervention and prevention strategies are often made in such a vacuum. The advantage of reviewing arrest reports and other supporting documentation in combination with data gathered from actual juvenile offenders is that it provides a rich tapestry from which to work. Of course, as Reiss and Roth (1993) mention, self-report surveys (we view our arson questionnaires as a type of self-report instrument) run the risk of not generating enough data for serious study. Although Reiss and Roth relate their concerns to the adequate study of serious and violent offenders, we think their point is well-taken.

Although no data source is without flaws, the Center for Arson Research has gathered enough material over the past twenty years from official sources, psychological and psychiatric assessments and firesetting evaluations to believe that the information is useful for the purposes of this chapter. The wealth of generic information about delinquency adds significantly to our body of knowledge overall, but adds little to our understanding of delinquent conduct that involves firesetting behavior. There is a lack of research that specifically leads us to recognize those factors in a youth's life that leads him or her to firesetting or that prohibits involvement in the behavior. The results of delinquency intervention programs do not generally measure what strategies lower the risk for firesetting. Candidly, we do not understand the reasons that cause some delinquents to abandon firesetting even if they continue to act out criminally in other ways. The final chapter of this text discusses the need for comprehensive, targeted research into firesetting behavior and offers recommendations for study.

Chapter 4

The Thought-disordered Firesetter

Russell's parents began to notice changes in him when he came home from college for Christmas break. He seemed different somehow—he didn't laugh at family reminiscences or hang around with his two younger brothers. He spent most of his time alone in his room and seemed "jumpy" at family get-togethers. He looked as though he lost weight and he declared that he was now on a strict diet to conserve the nation's food supply. He refused to answer the telephone or place any calls, claiming that computers could listen in and develop "voice prints as a dialectic." His parents reassured one another that Russell was going through a phase related to being away at school. After all, Russ really was a homebody; he never had strayed too far from his family growing up and he had always been a shy person. Russell denied that anything was wrong and he seemed irritated at his parents' concern for him. He told his brothers that he was "too busy" to do things with them, although he did not seem to be engaged in any activities that anyone could notice. He nailed his bedroom windows shut to keep out intruders. Russell's parents received a call late one night from the campus police shortly after Russ returned to school for spring semester. He had just been arrested for setting a fire in his dormitory that had caused considerable property damage and had resulted in injury to two students. Russell's parents rushed to the airport and flew across the country to the college town police station and found that Russ refused to see them. The police lieutenant informed them that Russell was proclaiming he was sent to save the world from invaders and that he was the true Captain Jack Black, pirate of the Caribbean. Russell had no previous contact with the criminal justice system, and outside of lighting campfires, had never displayed the slightest interest in setting fires.

For the purposes of this chapter, let us begin by defining what we mean by a thought disorder. A thought disorder is a condition in which associations lose their continuity so that thinking becomes bizarre, confused, and incorrect. Individuals suffering from a thought-disorder experience disturbances in verbal and motor behavior that affect their perceptual skills, thinking abilities, affective responses, and motivation (Wilson & Kneisl, 1983). Perception, as we speak of it here, relates to the cognitive and emotional knowing of an object or thought. Wilson and Kneisl observe that, although it is one of the most studied functions of human behavior, perception is also one of the least understood. In this chapter, we discuss the thought disorder of schizophrenia and apply our understanding of the disorder to the eleven subjects (4 percent) found among the 310 randomly selected individuals used for he purposes of this text.

Schizophrenia is a common mental health disorder throughout the world, generally characterized by the onset of symptoms in adolescence or young adult life. Individuals with schizophrenia are frequently stigmatized and their behavior often generates fear in the general public. Although considered a chronic disease, schizophrenia receives very little research attention despite it being the most expensive of all chronic illnesses. Torrey (1988) mentions that the cost of schizophrenia in this country is between ten to twenty billion dollars annually when one includes the cost of hospitalization, social security benefits, lost wages, and government subsidies. Often the person with schizophrenia suffers from a bizarre and frightening world, filled with perceptual distortions of hostile, mocking voices and disturbing thoughts, leaving little time for the external and real environment.

There are two primary types of perceptual disturbance: hallucinations and illusions. Hallucinations are perceptions that are false sensory impressions having no basis in reality; illusions are perceptual distortions of some real external stimuli. Perceptual distortion can occur in any one of the five senses: olfactory, tactile, gustatory, auditory, and visual. Auditory hallucinations are common in schizophrenia and generally are experienced as voices or conversations heard only by the listener. Visual, tactile, gustatory, and olfactory hallucinations are associated with some organic condition, such as drug intoxication or brain injury (Sommers-Flanagan & Sommers-Flanaghan, 2003).

There are a number of theories about the etiology of schizophrenia that, for convenience, can be grouped into two main schools of thought: biological and psychosocial. Some researchers believe that schizophrenia is not a single disease, but rather a collection of disorders with a number of common features (Cancro, 1983). Biological theories focus on possible chemical, genetic, and neuroanatomic influences. Biological abnormalities are thought to form the basis of problems with information processing, cognition, and perception commonly found in schizophrenia (Meltzer, 1987). Thought reflects reason, intellect, and judgment; whereas disintegration of thought is a hallmark of a thought-disorder diagnosis. Individuals who experience disturbance in their ability to think clearly most commonly have disintegration in the form, content, and flow of thought (Wilson & Kneisl, 1983).

Biological Theories

Twin studies have lent credence to the concept of genetic influences in schizophrenia. Studies of identical (monozygotic) twins demonstrate that if one twin develops schizophrenia, the incidence of the other twin developing it as well is three to six times higher than in fraternal (dizygotic) twins (Kallman, 1953). Other research has shown that children with one schizophrenic parent are more than 10 to 16 percent likely to develop schizophrenia than the general population. There is no central agreed-upon hypothesis around the mode of inheritance in schizophrenia although recent research suggests a connection between environmental stresses and a genetic susceptibility (Gottesman, et al., 1987).

Biochemical Theories

Understanding of brain chemistry continues to unfold as researchers develop increased ability to study brain processes, such as the neurotransmission of electric energy, metabolic changes in brain chemistry, neurochemistry, and blood flow in the brain. Cancro (1978) posits that there may be an altered ability to process sensory information in schizophrenics leading to sequelae, such as hypersensitivity, social isolation, and disturbances in attention. Ongoing studies of individuals diagnosed with schizophrenia indicate a failure in their ability to focus and sustain attention and direct their thoughts. Insignificant details in a situation appear to gain undue weight that are then incorporated into a delusional idea, directing the person's attention away from what is important (Anscombe, 1987).

The scope of this text precludes more than the most cursory of overviews into the complexity of studies related to biochemical influences on schizophrenia. Research into brain chemistry has fueled advances in medications available to treat symptoms that have constrained and ruined so many lives. It is beyond the scope of this text to explore the biochemical effects of psychotropic medications used in the treatment of schizophrenia. Readers interested in the subject will find pharmacologic texts available for review. Evidence of the direct causation between schizophrenia and any particular chemical brain system continues to remain elusive despite advances.

Neuroanatomic Theories

The increased ability to scan brain development and activity demonstrates impairment in a significant number of people diagnosed with schizophrenia (Seidman, 1983). Meltzer (1987) reports that structural abnormalities of the brain such as enlarged ventricles and asymmetries are detected via magnetic imaging scans in individuals at all stages of the disease. He also points out that frontal-lobe abnormalities detected in scans may account for some of the attentional and cognitive dissonance found in schizophrenia. Recent scientific advances underscore the hypothesis that schizophrenia may be the result of multiple causal factors, including altered brain chemistry and neuroanatomic abnormalities.

Psychosocial Theories

Andreasen and Carpenter, (1993) observe that schizophrenia is a highly complex and poorly understood disorder. A number of psychosocial vulnerability models exist that attempt to explain why certain individuals develop schizophrenia. One such model proposes that there is a predisposition in certain people who are unable to withstand excessive stress and break down under its weight. Those individuals have pre-morbid characteristics in their personalities, such as hypersensitivity, and social detachment that, under severe stress, convert to suspicion, withdrawal, and social isolation (Johnson,

1993). Research conducted by McGlashan (1989) identified several factors related to vulnerability to schizophrenia, including:

- impaired cognitive skills such as information processing, the ability to abstract thoughts and ideas, decreased attention span and the ability to differentiate relevant from irrelevant information,
- compromised psychophysiological abilities, including problems with sensory inhibitions and autonomic responsiveness to aversive stimuli, and
- poor coping skills, such as an inability to realistically assess the level of a perceived threat and the overuse of denial as a defense mechanism.

Faulty reaction to stress is a key characteristic in the vulnerability models for schizophrenia. Zubin (1980) suggested that schizophrenia is an episodic disorder triggered by highly-stressful life events in those individuals predisposed to psychosis. There are certain identified risk factors in this vulnerability theory, including poor economic status, social isolation, crowded living conditions, and minority status. The identification of the aforementioned variables is among the same factors used by social structure theorists to explain the causes of crime (Siegel, 2004). Table 4.1 compares demographic variables between thought disordered firesetters and all others.

Table 4.1
Demographic Variables of Thought-disordered Firesetters and All Other Subtypes

Variable	Thought-disordered	All Other Subtypes
Male	64%	91%
Female	36%	9%
White	73%	49%
Black	9%	44%
Hispanic	18%	5%
Other	0%	2%
Mean Age Firesetting (onset)	18 years	8 years
Mental Health History	40%	55%

Review of Table 4.1 reveals a number of interesting findings suggestive of the need for additional research. We, of course, recognize that such a small sample may not be necessarily meaningful but the writer notes that the findings related to the thought- disordered subtype ring true with other schizophrenic clients interviewed over the years. One of the most striking findings is the recognition that firesetting behavior in psychosis is not necessarily gender-driven, unlike firesetting behavior overall. Another finding worthy of additional study is that of the wide variance in racial groups related to thought-disordered firesetters. While it is clear that African Americans are overrepresented in mental institutions and prisons, it is also clear that as a group, African Americans do not seek mental health intervention until psychiatric hospitalization is necessary (Spector, 1979; Siegel, 2003). The data in this small sample suggests there may be an under representation related to requests for arson evaluations for minorities (all eleven adult subjects were either hospitalized or imprisoned at the time of their assessments). The findings by age also support the knowledge that schizophrenia generally has its onset in late adolescence or early adult life (Johnson, 1993).

Psychoanalytic theories maintain that the process for the development of schizophrenia develops very early in life. Freud (1952), the father of the psychoanalytic movement, believed that pressures resulting from relational problems between the mother and infant set the stage for trust and communication problems with others throughout life. Freud thought that such experiences in early life resulted in impaired ego development, affecting the ability to clearly understand events and interactions. Bartol (2002) notes that schizophrenia, perhaps due to its early onset, impacts on the affected individual socially and economically for a lifetime. Early exposure to a hostile or emotionally unavailable parent might produce an over-identification with those characteristics by the child who incorporates them into his or her own image and feels worthless and helpless (Arieti, 1976).

Erik Erikson (1968) proposed that schizophrenia develops when the child and parent do not develop mutual trust, making the child unable to trust himself or herself or form trusting relationships with others. Erikson identified eight stages of development encompassing infancy through old age. He hypothesized that each stage represented growth tasks that had to be successfully completed before the individual could move on to the next stage. The accomplishment of these life-tasks allows an individual to learn to cope with the stresses represented at each developmental stage.

Competence at mastery of the stages leads to maturity and the ability to handle stress and crisis, if presented. An overview of Erikson's developmental stages is found below in Table 4.2. The writer suggests that individuals suffering with schizophrenia do not experience competency at crisis and stress management.

Table 4.2
Erikson's Adaptive Development Stages Showing Maladaptive Characteristics at Each Stage

Infancy	
Trust	Mistrust
Oral Needs Met	Withdrawal
Adequate Mothering	
Acquisition of Hope	
Toddler	
Autonomy	Shame and Doubt
Self-Control and Self-Esteem	Low Self-Esteem
Good Will and Pride	Secretiveness
Rightful Dignity	Feelings of Persecution
Independence	
Sense of Justice	
Preschooler	
Initiative	Guilt
Loving	Hysterical Denial
Relaxed	Inhibition, Impotence, Paralysis
Bright in Judgment	Overcompensating by Showing Off
Energetic	Psychosomatic
Task-Oriented	Self-righteous, Moralistic
Adolescence	
Identity	Role Confusion
Idealistic	Delinquency
Fidelity	Doubt and Sexual Identity
Integration of Aptitudes with Opportunity	Over-identification with Cliques and Heroes
Confidence	

(continued)

Table 4.2
Erikson's Adaptive Development Stages Showing Maladaptive Characteristics at Each Stage *(continued)*

Young Adulthood	
Intimacy	Isolation
Commitment	Self-Absorption
Sacrifice	Distancing Behaviors
Compromise	Character Problems
Work Production	
Satisfactory Sex Relations	
Middle-Aged Adult	
Generatively	Stagnation
Guiding the Next Generation	Pseudo Intimacy
Productivity	Personal Impoverishment
Creativity	Self-Love
	Lack of Faith
Older Adult	
Integrity	Despair
Assurance of order and Meaning	Fear of Death
Unifying Life Philosophy	Sense of Time Gone By
Acquisition of Wisdom	Disgust
Emotional Integration	

Note: Based on information in "Childhood and society" BY e. Erikson, 1968.

Traditional psychological theories about schizophrenia were developed after social scientists studied those individuals already diagnosed with the disorder. Johnson (1993) observed that in the 1960's and 1970's, it was quite popular to blame the family for "causing" schizophrenia because of faulty communication patterns and impaired family relationships. Those hypotheses have fallen largely into disrepute, especially in light of current advances in knowledge about brain chemistry. Some theorists articulate a belief that the individual with schizophrenia is greatly affected by the attitudes of his or her family. This hypothesis, called expressed emotion, posits that individuals with schizophrenia fare better in families when their bizarre behavior is accepted as symptomatic of an illness rather than as deliberate (Brooker, 1990). To that end, families with a schizophrenic member are urged to manage the environment for the affected person who is seen as subject to extreme emotional sensitivity. Organizations, such as the National Alliance for the Mentally Ill, object to such a characterization of the role of the family. They offer the opinion that expressed-emotion theory once again places blame for the emergence of symptoms on the way the family expresses attitudes rather than on schizophrenia as a disease (Conn, 1990).

There are multiple subtypes of schizophrenia that offer features unique only to the subtype and serve to differentiate one from the other. The *Diagnostic and Statistical Manual of Mental Disorders*, forth edition, revised (DSM -IV), defines the subtypes of schizophrenia and the essential features of each are found below:

- **Paranoid type**—essential features include a preoccupation with delusions and/or hallucinations that reflect grandiosity or persecution. This subtype, of all the schizophrenias, is the one most represented in the criminal justice system (Batrol, 2002).
- **Disorganized type**—essential features include a flat, inappropriate or silly affect, along with a delusional system and extreme, disorganized behavior.
- **Catatonic type**—essential features include muscular rigidity, mutism, negativism or excitement.
- **Undifferentiated** type—essential features include hallucinations, delusions, along with confused and disorganized behavior. This subtype does not fit into any of the other subtypes.
- **Residual type**—essential features include a past history of schizophrenia, along with some current symptoms such as social withdrawal without a current psychosis

Generally speaking, the mentally ill are no longer institutionalized in long-term care facilities and those who are hospitalized or sent to a forensic unit are ultimately released. Teplin(1984) notes that those who would have previously been institutionalized for their aberrant and dangerous behavior are now filling our jails and prisons. An article in *Lancet* (Davis, 2003) mentions that there are three times as many mentally ill individuals in prison than in mental hospitals in the United States and that one in every six prisoners is mentally ill. Research, particularly before 1965, on the effects of stigmatizing mental illness consistently maintained that the seriously mentally ill were no more at risk to commit a crime of violence than any other member of society (Rabkin, 1979).

Studies that are more recent suggest that mentally ill males with at least one episode of violence in their histories will commit another act of violence within a year after discharge from a hospital (Monahan, 1992). Blackburn (1993) and Bartol (2003) note that schizophrenia is the mental illness most closely connected to violence although over 90 percent of individuals diagnosed with a serious mental illness are not violent (Monahan, 1992). Prisoners have significantly more medical and mental health problems than found in the general population. Siegel (2003) remarks that mentally ill prisoners (about 16 percent of the total inmate population) often have factors in their histories that place them at risk for violence, including overcrowded living conditions, past abuse, poverty, joblessness, lack of treatment for their conditions and substance abuse. Table 4.3 looks at a number of risk-related variables in the sample of firesetters.

In every variable listed above, the thought-disordered subjects appeared to suffer significantly more than other firesetters and had less hope for their futures. The findings of this small sample seem to support larger studies, including the recognition that substance abuse in the mentally ill

Table 4.3
Comparing Risk-related Variables in Schizophrenic Firesetters and All Others

Variable	Schizophrenic	All Others
Substance Abuse	73%	28%
Family Discord	91%	91%
Domestic Violence (exposure to)	73%	27%
Physical Abuse	36%	27%
Sexual Abuse	18%	9%
Emotional Abuse	27%	15%
Future Goals/Hope	27%	40%

is much higher than in the general population (Wagner, et al., 1994). The finding on substance abuse also suggests that drug and alcohol use is significantly higher in schizophrenic firesetters than in all other firesetters, taken as an aggregate. Research demonstrates that the arrest rates for the mentally ill with previous psychiatric hospitalizations are disproportionate to the general population of arrestees, especially for assault (Rabkin, 1979; Hochstedler Steury, 1993). The thoughtful review of the literature study by Rabkin determined that there were two possible explanations for the disproportion in rates. Firstly, she found that a small group of hospitalized offenders with antisocial conduct and criminal records continued their behavior after discharge from a psychiatric facility. Rabkin observed that psychiatric patients without a criminal history had significantly fewer arrests than the general population.

A second finding by Rabkin (1979) determined that the majority of criminal offenses after discharge were committed by individuals with previous diagnoses of substance abuse or personality disorders. Once those individuals were removed from the study, Rabkin found that arrest rates for discharged mental patients without a criminal history were comparable to the general population. However, when she reviewed collected study data for the years between 1965 and 1979, Rabkin (1979) determined that arrest rates for the mentally ill appeared to be greater than the general population for violent crimes against others. More recent work has identified a causal relationship between arrests and mental illness, particularly an active psychosis (Sosowsky, 1986). A ten year study by Henn and others looked at a sample of 1,195 defendants referred for psychiatric assessment. They discovered that approximately 40 percent of the offenders were diagnosed with a personality disorder while the second most common diagnosis was schizophrenia, at 17 percent (Henn, Herjanic, & Vanderpearl, 1976).

A number of studies of mentally ill offenders found a causal relationship between crimes of violence and the presence of delusions and hallucinations. Taylor and Gunn (1984) and Hafner and Boker (1982) interviewed mentally ill offenders and discovered that many acts of violence by the subjects were motivated directly or indirectly by the presence of hallucinations and delusions. Taylor (1998) determined that individuals who suffer from delusions act on them frequently and delusions of persecution are especially prone to incite acting out with violence (Wesley, et al., 1993).

Planansky and Johnston (1977) stated that if violence occurred, it happened during the active phase of psychosis.

Deliberate firesetting behavior is considered an act of violence, generally directed against property although humans and animals are also targets. As a component of the firesetting evaluation, all respondents are asked a series of questions related to motivation for the crime, without regard to the target. Supporting documentation was reviewed relative to the subjects of this study to determine if the responses to motivation matched. Unfortunately, relatively few assessments and other diagnostic evaluations captured the element of motivation. The motivation variables for firesetting behavior in the eleven schizophrenic subjects identified by the Center for Arson Research are compared to those variables in all other subtypes in Table 4.4.

Table 4.4
Comparing Primary Firesetting Motivation in Schizophrenic Firesetters and All Others

Variable	Schizophrenic	All Others
Revenge	0%	4%
Anger	18%	23%
Peers	0%	9%
Depression	18%	1%
Hallucinations/Delusions (at the time of the fires)	36%	0%
Accidental	18%	2%
Did Not Know	9%	27%
Boredom	0%	7%
Curiosity	0%	4%
Anxiety Relief	0%	3%
Other Crime Concealment	0%	1%
Denial of Arson	0%	9%
For Fun	0%	8%

Note: Accurate within < or > four percentage points.

Table 4.4 presents the percentages of reported motivation in the schizophrenic subtypes and compares those to all others. The eleven thought disordered (schizophrenic) subjects were alone in claiming "voices or/and thoughts" as their motivation to set fires. Interestingly, as a group, they accepted responsibility for their arson fires, while 9 percent of the other subtypes denied any firesetting behavior. Review of the table finds that the group "all others" acknowledged motivation for firesetting in all thirteen possible categories except for hallucinations/delusions. Interestingly, the schizophrenic group acknowledged motivation in five of the possible thirteen categories. The smallness of the sample prevents us from drawing any conclusions about the factor of motivation as it relates to the psychotic subtype, but it appears to support the research mentioned above regarding violence prevalence during the active psychotic phase.

We also turned our attention to the number of fires set, any planning of the fire event(s), along with whether the fires were a solitary activity. Table 4.5 demonstrates those results.

Table 4.5
Comparison of Number of Fires Set, Planning of the Fires, and Type of Activity

Fires Set	Schizophrenic	All Others
None	0%	4%
One-Five	82%	57%
Six-Nine	0%	4%
Ten or more	18%	15%
Unknown Number (many)	0%	18%
Fires Set Alone	64%	42%
Fires Set with Others	36%	27%
Both Alone and with Others	0%	20%
Denies Fires	0%	9%
Fires Planned	45%	17%
Accelerants Used	0%	24%

Note: Accurate within < or > two percentage points.

The majority of schizophrenic subjects acknowledged setting from one to five fires before their arrest or imprisonment while the remaining 18 percent claimed to have set ten or more fires before they were stopped. In comparison, 57 percent of all others admitted to setting from one to five fires while the remaining respondents were represented in the four other categories (none, six to nine fires, ten or more fires, unknown number). It is important to note that often respondents (sample subjects as well as clients in general) report fire activity previously unknown, or if known, unable to be successfully prosecuted, to authorities.

The thought-disordered subjects reported setting fires alone one and a half times more often than the all others group. This finding supports the general characteristic of social isolation and withdrawal associated with schizophrenia (Johnson, 1993). We confess to some surprise at the finding that 36 percent set fires with others and, frankly, did not expect the result. It is noted, however, that all eleven subjects set the fire leading up to arrest or hospitalization as a solitary act. We are uncertain about the contribution this small sample of eleven schizophrenic subjects makes to a greater understanding of firesetting as a solitary behavior.

A study by Harris and Rice (1996) of 243 men admitted to a maximum security psychiatric facility for firesetting sheds some additional light on the behavior of thought-disordered arsonists. They determined that the largest group of the 243 patient subjects were psychotic, primarily schizophrenic (33 percent), and set fires secondary to delusions. Additional findings from the Harris and Rice study include the discoveries that the psychotic subtype set few fires in their life times, had insignificant histories of aggression or involvement with the justice system, and were unlikely to have an alcohol problem. They were also unlikely to have used accelerants in their fires (a finding replicated in the Center for Arson Research sample).

The Center for Arson Research collects data on the feelings clients associate with the fire event. For our purposes, collecting data on feelings move us along in our attempt to solidify arsonist typologies. Our assumption is that patterns related to motivation, feelings, antecedent behaviors, and experiences emerge and underscore our belief that firesetters can and should be divided into subtypes. A look at feeling states associated with firesetting is presented below in Table 4.6. For the same purposes, we also collect information on where the idea to set fires originated, as best the clients are able to recall. Those results, presented in Table 4.7, provide us with some interesting information. We have not been able to find other research data on firesetting idea formation.

Review of the results indicate some interesting differences between the thought-disordered subtype and all others. It seems significant that more than half (55 percent) of the schizophrenic subjects attribute their idea to set fires to hallucinations and delusions while only 1.0 percent of all others claimed the same impetus. Of interest to us as clinicians is the number of subjects who claim not to remember where they got the idea to set fires originally. As it speaks to onset behavior of particular pathology, an understanding of the origin could be of benefit in designing treatment protocols.

Table 4.6
Comparing Feelings between Schizophrenic Firesetters and All Others

Variable	Schizophrenic	All Others
Anger	1%	10%
Depression	18%	5%
Scared/Nervous	18%	21%
Power/Excitement	0%	4%
Sorry/Remorseful	0%	5%
Intrigue	0%	2%
Happy/Relieved	9%	13%
Silly/Stupid	0%	10%
Boredom	18%	8%
Preoccupation/Confusion	18%	0%
Don't Know	18%	31%

Table 4.7
Comparing the Credited Idea of Origin between Schizophrenic Subjects and All Others

Variable	Schizophrenic	All Others
My Own Idea	0%	10%
Peers/Siblings	9%	17%
Media	0%	4%
Hallucinations/Delusions	55%	1%
Watching Other Firesetters	0%	2%
Parent(s)	0%	2%
Don't Remember	36%	54%
Unknown	0%	10%

It is clear that much work needs to be undertaken to further our understanding of the use of fire by psychotic offenders. One question we pose, theoretically, is whether schizophrenic arsonists are any more dangerous than non-firesetter offenders who are psychotic. In other words, does the presence of firesetting in the behavioral profile of a person with a psychosis indicate an increased risk of violence? Secondly, there appears a paucity of research about the re-emergence of firesetting in an individual who becomes non-compliant with medication. We are not certain if previously experienced delusions and hallucinations that guided firesetting behavior return, in one modified form or another, if the psychosis exacerbates. Finally, the more we understand about the relationship between psychosis, firesetting and community risk, the more helpful treatment providers will be to the mentally ill and society.

Interrogation Strategies for Police and Fire Investigators (hints from experience)

There are a number of points related to interrogation strategies to obtain information and affirmation of the crime of arson from a thought-disordered suspect. Central to questioning is the interrogator's understanding that psychosis is not a "game" played by the suspect to annoy or thwart the investigation. As it was discussed, a thought disorder interferes with cognition and the ability to reason soundly. It is not helpful, for instance, to advise a psychotic suspect to confess "for your own good" as the individual may lack the capacity to weigh options and arrive at a reasonable decision. The development of trust is essential in opening channels of communication between the suspect and investigators. We urge a non-judgmental, non-blaming attitude along with a demonstration of interest and concern. Your body language, facial expressions and language are evaluated by the suspect who, remember, is often filtering them through hallucinations and delusions. The impressions of individuals with a thought disorder, such as schizophrenia, are often very acute and they seem to "read" your true feelings about them. It is important for you to suspend judgment and focus on the immediate task, building some level of rapport. Establishing rapport is very important and you should count on interrogating the suspect a number of times in order to increase the person's trust in you.

It is best to appear non-threatening physically and mentally. Remember that if the suspect is in an active psychosis where he or she has symptoms, such as hearing voices, there is an increased possibility of agitation and aggression. The person's ability to follow your questions and respond meaningfully is extremely compromised. Language may be symbolic and sound nonsensical or confusing to the listener. A suspect in an active psychosis has a poor attention span, is a bad listener, and is easily overwhelmed by a high stress environment. If you bring someone with an active psychosis in for questioning, make your questions short, concrete, and easy to follow. Find out as quickly as possible if the suspect takes any psychotropic medication regularly. If not, the individual's capability to follow and comprehend your questions is compromised significantly. Keep your interrogation sessions short and make up in frequency what you lack in intensity. Be aware of what the individual can tolerate.

Do not sit too close or lean in, since many who suffer from a thought disorder have spatial distortion problems, so you may appear closer than you are and seem threatening. Do not join in any psychotic ideas, as in "So you think you're the devil. Well, we agree with you." Be careful not to touch the suspect; paranoid schizophrenics may perceive a touch as a physical or sexual attack and respond with fear or aggression. Set up your interview space to reflect as little stimulation as possible. Plain clothes are often more effective than uniforms which can reinforce feelings of persecution and increase hostility (Johnson, 1993). Be aware of the potential for violence in the suspect and determine whether the individual has the capacity to monitor his or her feelings and control behavior. It is best to maintain a neutral position as the interrogator, neither friendly nor antagonistic, and remain alert for clues and cues regarding the suspect's thoughts and emotions.

Chapter 5

The Revenge Firesetter

Christopher grew up in a family that had one basic philosophy of dealing with the world and that was to "never get taken advantage of" by other people. Chris' father, in particular, taught him to be very suspicious about the motivations of others and often told him, "You got family so you don't need friends. Blood is thicker than water, anyway." Throughout school, Chris had very few friends and other kids mostly avoided him. His reputation was one of having a hair-trigger temper and everybody knew not to tease him because he could not take a joke and responded with aggression. Chris never had a date to anyone's knowledge. The quote under his yearbook picture was, "Don't get mad, get even." After graduation from high school, he entered the Army because he liked their phrase, "An Army of One". He became a Special Forces ranger and was trained in demolitions. Chris frequently got into trouble for insubordination and was resentful of orders from "...those higher ups who don't know s—." He was particularly resentful of one officer who he believed was out to get him. One night, after an off-base drinking episode, Chris attacked the officer and beat him severely, causing a concussion and several fractures. Chris was court-martialed and discharged from the service. In recognition of his bravery in a number of military battles, he was not imprisoned, but did lose all his military benefits. After the service, Chris grew more reclusive and angry. He was bitter about what he considered unfair treatment by the Army and often talked when he was drinking about living in another country. He moved frequently, going from job to job (generally as a security guard), often finding fault with co-workers and supervisors. He took a job as a night watchman at a utility company, "Because that way, idiots leave you the hell alone." He had unstable relations with women, featuring

65

Chris' pronounced sexual entitlement and aggressive style, along with a lack of emotional connectedness. Christopher drank heavily and amassed multiple absences at work, leading to a formal reprimand and warning of termination. He considered this warning as a deliberate persecution by the human resource director against him. After several more "no-shows" on his shift, Chris was fired. During the termination meeting, he threatened the human resource director, telling him, "You'll be sorry that you ever met me. I wouldn't try to start my car, if I was you." Christopher was escorted off the premises by security and the police were notified. The company took Chris' threat to heart and for the next week, security made frequent rounds in the parking lot and kept their eyes open for any signs of Chris. When, after several weeks, nothing happened, everyone relaxed. Five weeks after being fired, Chris, wearing camouflage clothing, entered the unsecured parking lot and poured gasoline on the seats of the human service director's car. He tossed a match and stepped back. When apprehended outside the building, Chris was armed with a semiautomatic handgun and four ammunition clips. He commented, "The f——— should be glad he wasn't in the car." He denied the intent to shoot anyone, "I wanted him to have a wake up call".

Revenge arsonists set fires as an act of retaliation against another individual or entity for some real or imagined wrong. A study by Sapp, Huff, Gary, and Icove (1994) divides the revenge arsonist into four additional categories: personal, societal, institutional, and group, based upon the arson target. For the purposes of this chapter, we regard revenge arsonists, as a whole, irrespective of the target. The study by Sapp et al. (1994) determined that revenge arsonists are almost always single, white males with an average ten years of education and poor school performance. The Sapp group found that revenge arsonists were generally middle class with intact, but emotionally distant, families. As a type, they found revenge firesetters to have histories of misdemeanor and felony arrests. Sapp et al. also noted that the revenge arsonists they studied had histories of psychiatric inpatient admissions.

Sapp et al. (1994), studying arsonists at the request of the National Center for the Analysis of Violent Crime (NCAVC), concluded that revenge arsonists set an average of thirty-five fires, generally to non-residential structures, before apprehension and conviction. When arrested, revenge arsonists admit responsibility for their behavior, and blame others for the necessity of the crime. The researchers discovered age fifteen to be the average age of onset in revenge firesetting behavior, a finding supported by the Center for Arson Research study. Sapp et al. also determined that revenge fires are targeted, pre-meditated, solitary, and intentional. Interestingly, Sapp et al. found that revenge arsonists do nothing to avoid discovery and do not consider the possibility of arrest as a deterrent. They do not follow their cases in the media and appear to lose interest after the crime is committed. If interrogated, revenge arsonists are questioned, on the average, five times before confessing (Sapp et al., 1994).

The Center for Arson Research identified forty-seven subjects (15 percent) of a total 310 as fitting the profile of the revenge firesetter. Table 5.1 reveals general characteristics of this subtype. The mean age of onset for firesetting behavior in this sample is ten years in comparison to the Sapp et al. study that found age fifteen as the average onset age. Interestingly, 13 percent of the revenge arsonists in the Center for Arson Research sample are female. The mean age of subjects evaluated by the Center for Arson Research was fifteen years.

Review of supportive documentation obtained as a component of conducting firesetting evaluations on the forty seven revenge arsonists in the Center for Arson Research study found commonalities in their histories. The male subjects were described overall as suspicious, hostile, emotionally guarded, and distant. They experienced their treatment in the

Table 5.1
General Characteristics of the Revenge Firesetter

Variable	Number	Percentage
Male	41	87%
Female	6	13%
White	16	34%
Black	26	55%
Hispanic	3	6%
Other	2	4%
Juvenile Justice History	15	32%
Adult Criminal History	8	17%

world as unfair and expressed the opinion that they were prevented from achieving their life goals by some authority figure or entity. As adolescents, the subjects most often carried the diagnosis of conduct disorder or oppositional defiant disorder and as adults, antisocial or paranoid personality disorder. We will examine each diagnosis in turn; antisocial personality disorder is described in chapters six and seven.

There is an inherent difficulty in distinguishing normal adolescent behavior from psychological disturbance, but if a true condition exists, there is small chance that the youth will just outgrow it (Moore, 1981). One study suggests that about 20 percent of adolescents experience psychological problems severe enough to interfere with functioning, another 20 percent have no discernable mental health problems and 60 percent have some occasional problems with anxiety and depression, but still function without major dysfunction (Weiner, 1982).

Approximately one million teenagers runaway from home each year and over half of all serious crimes, including arson, are committed by youth between the ages of ten to seventeen (Huba, Wingard & Bentler, 1979; Stein & Freidlich, 1975; Williams, 1988). Studies reveal that about 5 percent of adolescents between ages fourteen to eighteen have a serious substance abuse problem (Johnson, 1993). Another study determined that early drunkenness is a risk factor in predicting drug abuse and major depression (Deykin, Levy & Wells, 1987). A study by Loeber, Green, Keenan and Lahey (1995), however, found that substance misuse in preadolescents was not a predictor of conduct disorder in adolescence. An interesting study by Brown, Glegham, Schuckit, Myers, and Mott (1996) examined whether symptoms of conduct disorder pre or post dated substance abuse (primarily alcoholism) in 166 adolescent males. The group whose negative behaviors predated substance abuse (48 percent) had a significantly earlier onset of conduct disorder symptoms as well as some behaviors not usual in the general population, such as setting fires and cruelty to animals. Table 5.2 examines a number of the aforementioned risk-related variables. In almost every category, revenge firesetters have a significantly increased response to the factors related to serious mental health problems.

In general, youth diagnosed with a mental health disorder are at increased risk for poor outcome in adult life (Östman, O., 1991). A number of studies have found a substantive link between a diagnosis related to disrup-

Table 5.2
Comparing Risk Variables Between Revenge Firesetters
and All Other Subtypes

Variable	Revenge	All Other Subtypes
Depression	53%	31%
Runaway	53%	32%
Behavior Problems (home and school)	64%	56%
Substance Abuse (self)	43%	27%
Substance Abuse (parent)	30%	39%
Mental Health History	43%	40%
Cruelty to Animals	17%	14%

tive behavior in childhood and adolescence and a diagnosis of personality disorder in adulthood (Moffitt, 1993; Kasen, Cohen, Skodol, Johnson & Brook, 1999). Attention deficit hyperactive disorder (ADHD), the leading psychological disorder for American children (about 3 percent of the population and primarily male), according to Cowley (1993) is frequently associated with a diagnosis of conduct disorder (Reid, 1993). ADHD has three central behaviors: inattention and distractibility, impulsivity, and excessive motor activity. Although there continues to be debate about the exact cause of ADHD, many believe it to be a combination of biochemical, genetic, environmental, and neurological factors (Weiss, 1990).

According to Moffitt and Silva (1988), there seem to be links between ADHD and family turmoil while a number of studies associate ADHD with the onset of delinquency and adult criminal conduct. Although ADHD is popularly thought to disappear with adulthood, growing evidence supports the thesis that the main features of hyperactivity exist throughout adult life (Klinteberg, Magnussan, & Schalling, 1989). Youth who carry the ADHD diagnosis tend to annoy and frustrate others and often face rejection by peers because of their irritating and intrusive behavior (Henker & Whalen, 1989). Data suggest that youth diagnosed with ADHD who also engage in delinquent behavior at early ages present a very high risk for serious and lengthy criminal careers (Farrington, 1991; Moffitt, 1990). Table 5.3 identifies key behavioral symptoms of attention deficit hyperactive disorder.

Table 5.3
Key Behavioral Symptoms in ADHD

- Short attention span.
- Easily distracted by external stimuli.
- Does not listen well.
- Repeatedly fails to follow through on instructions, school assignments, or responsibilities.
- Poor organizational skills.
- Hyperactivity with restlessness, loud talking, and difficulty sitting still.
- Impulsivity demonstrated by an inability to take turns, intrusiveness, and blurting out answers to questions before they are fully asked.
- Frequent disruptive, aggressing, or negative attention-seeking behavior.
- Poor social skills.
- Careless and dangerous behavior.

Note: Adopted from information in, "The child and adolescent psychotherapy treatment planner" by A. Jongsma, M. Peterson & W. McInnis, 1996

It is estimated that approximately 40 percent of youth diagnosed with ADHD will develop a conduct disorder while substance abuse, depression, and anxiety are also fairly common (Lock, 1996). Conduct disorder refers to a set of constant behaviors that are socially disapproved. According to the DSM-IV (1994), the primary feature of a conduct disorder is repetitive and persistent behavior that violates others' rights. As young children, conduct disordered youth are often in trouble, first at home and then in school, with behaviors that retain continuity into adult life. Because they have difficulty completing school assignments, conduct disordered children and adolescents are mislabeled frequently as suffering from a learning disability (Reid, 1993). The etiology of conduct disorder is unknown, but is believed to arise from a combination of psychological and social-environmental factors. If severe behavioral symptoms of conduct disorder last into adulthood, the diagnosis changes to antisocial personality disorder (Lock, 1996).

Approximately 9 percent of males and 2 percent of females are thought to have symptoms of conduct disorder (Zoccoulillo, 1993; Maxmen & Ward, 1995). Conduct disordered behavior can include such criminal activities as property damage, arson, theft, assault, and murder, as well as non-criminal conduct, such as acting out in school, bullying and lying (Straker, 1979). Youth with a conduct disorder behave as though they are adults. They have early sexualized behavior with multiple partners and engage in smoking, drinking, and using drugs from a young age (Maxim & Ward, 1995). The DSM-IV (1994) identifies two types of conduct disorders: childhood onset, with a pattern of behavior beginning prior to age ten and adolescent onset, with a pattern of behavior beginning after age ten. There is a more favorable prognosis for those youth with a later age onset. Table 5.4 describes the DSM-IV criteria for conduct disorder.

Many social scientists and mental health providers consider oppositional defiant behavior a precursor to a conduct disorder. Oppositional defiant conduct includes disrespect and hostility towards authority figures, as well as disobedience with rules, temper tantrums and displays of spite, anger, and resentment (Jongsma et al., 1996, pp. 113-114). Their negative behavior is always present at home but may not be in evidence at school or with anyone other than family. Maxmen and Ward (1995) note that the most flagrant misbehavior is reserved for people they know very well. What sets these youth apart from those with conduct disorder is that, although annoying and hostile, they do not seriously violate anyone's rights or social mores. The etiology of oppositional defiant disorder is not clearly understood but results, most probably, from the same set of individual psychological and social environmental factors as does conduct disorder. Table 5.5 lists the criteria for oppositional defiant disorder.

Clients interviewed by the Center for Arson Research frequently are diagnosed with opositional defiant disorder, in childhood, or conduct disorder, in adolescence. Table 5.6 reviews selected variables associated with oppositional defiant disorder and conduct disorder and compares the findings in the revenge and all other subtypes. Most commonly, requesters of firesetting evaluations do not regard motivation as of primary importance. Rather, firesetting often seems to be regarded as a serious and dangerous manifestation of delinquency or alternately, as a prank gone wrong.

Table 5.4
DSM-IV Criteria for Conduct Disorder

A. A repetitive and persistent pattern of behavior in which the basic rights of others or major age-appropriate societal norms or rules are violated, as manifested by the presence of three, or more, of the following criteria in the past twelve months with at least one criterion preset in the past six months.

- Aggression towards people and animals.
  - Often bullies, threatens, or intimidates others.
  - Often initiates physical fights.
  - Has used a weapon that can cause serious physical harm.
  - Has been physically cruel to people.
  - Has been physically cruel to animals.
  - Has stolen while confronting a victim.
  - Has forced someone into sexual activity.

- Destruction of property.
  - Has deliberately engaged in firesetting with the intention of causing serious damage.
  - Has deliberately destroyed others' property (other than by firesetting).

- Deceitfulness or theft.
  - Has broken into someone's home, business, or car.
  - Often lies to obtain goods or favors to avoid obligations.
  - Has stolen items of non-trivial value without confronting a victim (e.g., shoplifting).

- Serious violation of rules.
  - Often stays out at night despite parental prohibitions, beginning before age thirteen.

B. The disturbance in behavior causes clinically significant impairment in social, academic, or occupational functioning.

Note: Adopted from the DSM-IV, pp. 90-91

Table 5.5
DSM-IV Criteria for Oppositional Defiant Disorder

A. A pattern of negative, hostile, and defiant behavior lasting at least six months, during which four or more of the following are present:

- Often loses temper.
- Often argues with adult.
- Often actively defies or refuses to comply with adult requests or rules.
- Often deliberately annoys people.
- Often blames others for behavior or mistakes.
- Is often touchy or easily annoyed.
- Is often angry and resentful.
- Is often spiteful or vindictive.

B. The behavioral disturbance causes clinically significant impairment in social, academic, or occupational functioning.

C. The behaviors do not occur exclusively during a psychotic or mood disorder.

D. Criteria are not met for conduct disorder and, if eighteen or older, criteria are not met for antisocial personality disorder.

Note: Adopted from the DSM-IV, pp. 93-94

Review of Table 5.6 reveals a number of interesting findings, among them that in most variables related to conduct disorder or oppositional defiant disorder, revenge firesetters score significantly higher than their counterparts. Although delinquent firesetters often carry the same mental health diagnoses as revenge firesetters, they do not appear as dysfunctional or damaged on paper or in person (refer to Chapter 3 for review of delinquent firesetting behavior). Bartol (2002) mentions that, contrary to what often is written about delinquents, few mental health providers really believe them to be emotionally disturbed and in need of conventional psychotherapy. Bartol notes that many contemporary clinicians view delinquent conduct as learned behavior, rather than psychological maladjustment.

Table 5.6
**Comparing Certain Variables in Revenge Firesetters
and All Other Subtypes**

Variable	Revenge	All Other Subtypes
ADHD Diagnosis	59%	72%
Behavior Problems (home, school, community)	56%	64%
Impulsivity	84%	94%
Chronic Lying	79%	87%
Theft/Shoplifting	49%	60%
Fighting	63%	72%
Property Destruction (non-fire)	58%	68%
Problems with Authority	38%	45%
Learning Problems	55%	57%
Friends	50%	57%
Sexually Active	29%	36%
Family Discord	76%	74%
One or Both Parents Absent	70%	62%
Truancy	21%	23%
Remorse for Behavior	20%	30%
Suicide Attempts	14%	30%
Feels Angry Most of the Time	64%	81%

The literature suggests that youth who are diagnosed as oppositional defiant or conduct disordered generally escalate their asocial behavior during adolescence. Because of increased truancy, an active dislike of the educational environment, poor school performance, and continued negative behaviors, many teens are expelled or drop out of school before graduation (Robins & McEvoy, 1990). Adolescents who have a conduct disorder may continue to experience low self-esteem and feelings of depression, sometimes accompanied by thoughts or attempts of suicide. Research indicates that youth battling a conduct disorder through adolescence often continue their behaviors into adulthood, developing antisocial personalities and criminal records (Kazdin, 1985). Some social scientists posit that youth who exhibit diffuse aggressive behavior in childhood present a high risk to develop antisocial conduct later on in life (Satterfield et al., 1995).

Although there are a variety of therapeutic approaches for the treatment of conduct disorder, interventions are not generally very successful, according to Wells and Egan (1988). Children and youth with oppositional defiant and conduct disorder exhibit a wide range of behavioral and attitudinal symptoms making it relatively impossible to design a "one size fits all" intervention strategy. Many youth who experience such severe disruptive behavior carry multiple chronic life stressors, such as poverty, parental addictions, and histories of abuse. In fact, there is conflict about whether conduct disorder is actually a psychiatric condition as so many youth with the diagnosis exist in marginalized families with severe sociological problems (Johnson, 1993). Short-term intervention that only focuses on the youth's behavior does little to provide any lasting change (Yoshikawa, 1994). Clinicians believe that the family system must be altered to bring about any real change in the behavior of a youth with conduct or oppositional defiant disorders.

The study of youth who develop a conduct disorder indicates that about 25 percent of them grow up to develop adult personality disorder, according to Lock (1996) while the others continue into adulthood with serious, ongoing problems. Lock notes that, as adults, many adolescents with a conduct disorder experience psychotic disorders, substance abuse problems, depression, poor work and relationship histories, and financial problems. Substance abuse is the most common secondary disorder associated with conduct disorder and features in acts of delinquency. Longitudinal studies have demonstrated that impulse-related problems in childhood and adolescence increase the risk for alcohol abuse in adulthood (Schuckit, 1998).

Subjects in the Center for Arson Research study self report that 27 percent of the total cohort, excluding revenge firesetters, abuse drugs or alcohol or both while 43 percent of the revenge subtype report substance abuse histories. Delinquent firesetters are more likely than any other firesetting subtype to disclose a pattern of alcohol and drug use while with peers. Some delinquents report that their substance abuse relates to the desire to be impressive to their peers or to be part of the activity of the group. The peer influence theory proposes that teens use drugs in order to gain acceptance by their peers and fail to consider any possible long-term consequences of their behavior, not too surprising, considering the nature of adolescence (Kandel, D., Kessler, R., & Marguiles, R, 1978).

A second model concerned with the development of substance abuse is parental influence theory. This theory posits that youth who have negative relationships with parents are more susceptible to substance use, particularly alcohol, than youth with positive family relationships (Forslund, M. & Gustafson, T., 1970). The Center for Arson Research sample (see Table 5.7) reveals a number of interesting findings related to family dynamics. It is clear that over half of subjects in the research for this textbook suffered from some degree of trauma related to home and family life.

There is a richness of literature available pointing to the impact adverse family life has on the normal development of children (e.g. Guerra, Huesmann, Tolan, Van Acker, & Eron, 1995; Tolan & Thomas, 1995; Weiner, 1982). Exposure to family violence and constant disruption, poor or absent parenting skills, and substance abuse in adults limit a child's ability to develop adequate interpersonal or social skills, let alone good values. Heide (1995) notes that youth who kill their parents or stepparents typically come from homes where child abuse, domestic violence, and substance abuse are common. The sequelae of violence and substance abuse have a direct, long lasting, and negative impact on children. Emery (1989) discusses the impact that neglect and abuse can produce in childhood, citing their link to physical, cognitive, and emotional development. The nature and impact of abuse is discussed comprehensively in Chapter 7.

Table 5.7
Comparing Family-related Variables in Revenge Firesetters and All Other Subtypes

Variable	Revenge	All Other Subtypes
Family Discord	74%	76%
Domestic Violence	26%	30%
Absent Mother	2%	9%
Absent Father	32%	41%
Absent both Parents	20%	28%
Substance Abuse (parent)	30%	39%
Physical Abuse	30%	27%
Emotional Abuse	17%	15%
Sexual Abuse	6%	10%
All Three Abuses	3%	6%

As mentioned earlier in this chapter, paranoid personality disorder is also a common diagnosis of those clients arrested for an act of revenge firesetting. Johnson (1993, p. 425) describes paranoid personality as applying to an individual who experiences pervasive and long-standing suspiciousness. The individual perceives the world in a different way and is constantly alert for clues as to the "real" meaning of verbal or behavioral messages from others. Kraepelin, a psychiatrist, described a type of personality as one who "was always on the alert to find a grievance, but without delusions" (Kraepelin, 1905, p. 309). At the time of Kraepelin's identification of a paranoid personality, he and most of his colleagues conceptualized mental illnesses as physically based diseases with specific symptoms, in the same manner that physical illnesses were understood. Emil Kraepelin, (1856-1926), contributed enormously to the field of psychiatry by developing the first comprehensive classification system of mental illness. This system, with some modification to allow for psychological or environmental causation, is still in use today.

Kraepelin (1905) determined that an individual with a paranoid personality actively mistrusted others and tended to view himself as alone and an object of hostility and trickery. A person with such a mind-set sees the world as a threatening and deceitful environment. The individual's view of himself is narcissistic and markedly different from his perception of others. He believes himself to be objective, rational, powerful, intelligent and very important. This deluded self-perception helps the person to defend against low self-esteem (Marin, 1975). An individual with paranoid personality disorder tends to think in terms of rank and hierarchy, as in who is most important in any setting. Table 5.8 outlines the essential features of paranoid personality disorder.

The perceptual distortion found in someone with a paranoid thinking style has a profound impact on cognition. Such individuals tend to collect injustices they believe are directed deliberately at them. Johnson (1993) describes paranoid individuals as having cognitive disturbances that range from mild ideas of reference to mild delusional states reflecting either ideas of persecution or grandiose self-perception. They perceive themselves as having enemies and interact in a most unpleasant manner with others, causing people to avoid them. The avoidance reinforces the paranoid individual's perception that people are unfriendly and devious and the cycle is completed. If anyone attempts to communicate a feeling to someone with this personality disorder, he or she is regarded either as weak or up to something.

Table 5.8
Features of Paranoid Personality Disorder

A. A pervasive distrust and suspiciousness of others, such that their motives are interpreted as malevolent, beginning by early adulthood and present in a variety of contexts, indicated by at least four of the following:

- Suspects, without sufficient basis, that people are exploiting, harming, or deceiving him/her.
- Is preoccupied with unjustified doubts about the loyalty or trustworthiness of friends or associates.
- Is reluctant to take others into confidence for fear the information will be used maliciously.
- Reads hidden, demeaning, or threatening messages into benign encounters or happenings.
- Bears grudges.
- Easily perceives attacks on his/her reputation or character when none is intended.
- Is unjustifiably suspicious of the fidelity of sexual partner or spouse.

Note: Adopted from the DSM-IV, pp. 637-638

People with this disorder rarely enter treatment because they do not believe they have any faults or problems. Maxmen and Ward (1995) state that if a paranoid person is somehow coerced into therapy, the individual is very reluctant to provide any personal information to the therapist. There is no "bonding" between client and clinician and the relationship is adversarial rather than therapeutic. As a group, individuals with a paranoid personality disorder are quick to sue for imagined injury or inadequate care. Their general affect is that of extreme suspiciousness, heightened vigilance, profound mistrust and an inability to feel empathy for others. Millon (1981) divided the personality profile of an individual with a paranoid disorder into four categories: behavioral characteristics of vigilance, counterattack and marked irritability; complaints that signify oversensitivity; social isolation and mistrust; a coping style that exaggerates self-sufficiency and hostile distancing; and denial of personal insecurities along with grandiose fantasies about their own powers and worth.

Individuals with paranoid personality disorder believe themselves to be right and others to be wrong. They feel fully justified in their actions and do not apologize or explain. Cameron (1963) determined that many people with paranoid thinking patterns were treated abusively during childhood. That maltreatment created an inability for the individual to trust others and caused the person to develop the expectation of harm and deceit. Cameron identified four aspects to the paranoid personality: hypersensitivity towards others; lack of insight into one's own motivations; secret thoughts about sexual inferiority; along with poor self-esteem and unconscious guilt. Johnson (1993) posits that such individuals control their anxiety by projecting unwanted emotions and attributes onto others. Meissner (1979) believes that paranoia arises from a desperate attempt by an individual to increase self-esteem and control an environment perceived as hostile and chaotic.

Children learn behavior, attitudes, and values through exposure to caring adults. Such experiences teach children concepts related to trust and unconditional love which help to develop self esteem. Loving adults place limits on allowable behaviors and help children understand reasonable consequences for unacceptable conduct. Through this process, children begin to gain the skills necessary to live successfully in a civilized society (Unell & Wyckoff, 1995). Individuals who exhibit symptoms of paranoid personality disorder often grow up in homes where family discord and cruelty are the norm. Infants and very young children growing up in such toxic environments experience frustration and anxiety over unmet needs and they do not sense unconditional love. Such children exposed to cruelty and domestic violence grow up believing they will never find love, according to Jacobson (1971) setting the stage for mistrust and hostile interactions with others.

It is clear that there are differences in the perceptions and attitudes of subjects in the revenge subtype in comparison to all other subtypes. Table 5.9 compares selected variables, including firesetting motivation. The reader is advised that the motivation variables are not comprehensively listed for all other subtypes when the value for revenge firesetters was less than 1 percent. Exceptions were made for the variables of "peers" and "for relief" as both zero responses in the revenge subtype help to underscore their lack of emotional connectedness to self or others.

Table 5.9
Comparing Selected Behavioral Variables Between Revenge Firesetters and All Other Subtypes

Variable	Revenge	All Other Subtypes
Remorse for Behavior	30%	20%
Homicide Thoughts	17%	7%
Homicide Attempts	4%	1%
Seeks Revenge if Wronged	40%	13%
Motive for Firesetting (reported if $\geq 1\%$)	—	—
Anger	55%	17%
Revenge	19%	2%
Impress Peers	0%	6%
For Fun	4%	8%
For Relief	0%	3%
From Boredom	2%	8%
Suicide Attempt	2%	2%
Don't Know/Won't Say	18%	27%

Note: Accurate within < or > two percentage points.

While ten of the 263 non-revenge firesetter subjects denied setting fires, only one of the forty-seven revenge setters denied any firesetting activity. There are other differences found in the firesetting behavior of revenge firesetters from other subtypes. Table 5.10 looks at variables related to number of fires set and whether the behavior was a solitary act. The majority of firesetters in revenge and all others subtypes self-report that the majority of their fire activity was restricted to five or fewer deliberately set fires. (Note: This question does not take into account the size or location of the fire, but records only the activity itself). Face-to-face evaluations of firesetter subjects consistently reveal that most firesetters recall the number and location of their fires even long after the events took place.

Over half of revenge setters in the sample set fires alone while 40 percent of all others set fires as a solitary activity. Significantly more revenge firesetters (26 percent) sometimes set fires alone and sometimes with others while 18 percent of all others mixed solitary and peer-accompanied

Table 5.10
**Comparing Firesetting Variables Related to Numbers of Fires Set
and Participants in Revenge Firesetters and All Other Subtypes**

Variable	Revenge	All Other Subtypes
One-Five Fires Set	64%	55%
Six-Nine Fires Set	9%	3%
Ten-plus fires Set	24%	29%
Unknown Number of Fires Set	2%	9%
Fires Set Alone	60%	40%
Fires Set with Others	6%	31%
Fires Set Alone and with Others	26%	18%
No Response	6%	7%

firesetting. More research should be conducted to determine the dynamics specifically related to the determinants of solitary versus joined firesetting behavior. We suggest, based upon interviews over the years, revenge setters are more likely to engage in acts of firebombing or firesetting with others than as a solitary activity. Our experience as forensic interviewers leads us to believe that firebombing begins most commonly in adolescent revenge setters who begin experimentation with incendiaries and explosives during latency. In fact, when we work with school authorities, we reinforce our understanding that threats made with specificity to "blow up" some target should be taken seriously as a behavioral intent rather than as an idle threat. Review of the data collected for this study reveals that 22 percent of the revenge subjects self-reported they knew how to construct bombs and incendiaries while only 5 percent of the remaining 263 subjects reported bomb-making knowledge.

The study also looked at the subjects' understanding about the origins of their firesetting behavior (a variable understudied in the literature) as well as emotions they associated with the act of firesetting. Table 5.11 looks at that data. The ability to identify the origin of firesetting behavior information would assist in clarifying the use and importance of fire as a tool for acting out. The majority of subjects in the study declared that they had no idea where the idea originated; often commenting that it was a "long time" since it started. Two observations arising from the data include almost

Table 5.11
Origins of Firesetting and Emotions Associated with Firesetting in Revenge Firesetters and All Other Subtypes

Variable: Origin of Firesetting	Revenge	All Other Subtypes
Own Idea	15%	8%
Peer/Sibling	9%	18%
Media	9%	3%
Hallucinations/Delusions	2%	3%
Don't Know	55%	52%
Modeling Another Person	2%	2%
No Response	7%	12%
Parent/Other Adult	0%	2%
Variable: Emotions Associated with Firesetting		
Anger	28%	5%
Depression	9%	5%
Scared and Nervous	13%	21%
Power/Excitement	0%	4%
Shock	2%	0%
Relief	15%	11%
Interested	0%	3%
Stupid	2%	8%
Remorse	2%	5%
Boredom	6%	9%
Don't Know	17%	34%
Denial	2%	2%

double the number of revenge setters than all others claimed that setting fires was their idea, something they thought up all on their own. Conversely, all other subtypes attributed their idea to set fires as originating from peers or siblings at double that of revenge setters.

The two most common emotions associated with firesetting by revenge setters were anger (28 percent) and relief (15 percent) while 17 percent claimed that they did not know their feelings at the time of the events. In comparison, all other subtypes described their most common feelings to be that of being scared or nervous (21 percent) or relief at 11 percent. A significantly larger percentage of all other subtypes (34 percent), when compared to revenge setters, claimed not to know their feelings at the time of their fires. The lack of awareness of emotion pre-firesetting (or resistance to disclosure) has implications for treatment. The ability to identify feelings is instrumental in teaching the individual positive behavioral substitutes for firesetting when the emotion is experienced or desired.

There is a need for additional research into the development and motivation of those bent on revenge. A case can be made that the motivation of revenge is a factor in the behavior of certain terrorists. Nothing makes this need to understand purposeful destruction more strongly than the terroristic events of September 11, 2001.

Terrorism is defined as the unlawful use of force or violence against persons or property to intimidate or coerce a government, the civilian population, or any segment thereof, in furtherance of a political or social objective may be domestic or international (US Department. of Justice, 2000). Central to the cause of the terrorists is the use of the media to attract attention to the message (Adler, Mueller & Laufer, 1998). Before the attacks of September 11th, the deadliest incident of terrorism on US soil occurred when Timothy McVeigh bombed the Murrah Federal building in 1995, killing 168 people.

The FBI classifies terrorists according to their targets, ideology, and goals. An in-depth analysis of international and domestic terrorism is beyond the mission of this text and we review the topic only to provide an overview for the reader. Terrorists frequently employ the use of bombing, arson, and kidnapping to accomplish their mission, whatever it might be. It is not far-fetched to assume that an act of terrorism occurs somewhere every day of the year. Siegel (2003) describes the most common forms of terrorism, found below:

- **Revolutionary terrorism**—according to Siegel, the ultimate goal of this type of terrorist is to replace an existing government with one in support of the terrorists' political and religious views. An example is that of Islamic fundamentalists committed to oust any Western influence from a country or state. Siegel (2003) mentions the efforts of Muslim extremists who continue to target the tourist industry in Egypt in an attempt to drive out tourism and create a chaotic and unstable government to be replaced by an Islamic state.

- **Political terrorism**—Siegel notes that political terrorists direct their activities against those who disagree with their ideologies. Such political terrorists (generally white, blue-collar workers who are well-armed) in this country believe that their fundamental rights are eroding. Their view of the government is highly suspicious and they tend to organize around some central theme such as the right to bear arms or white supremacy. In 1996, agents of Alcohol, Tobacco and Firearms uncovered a plot by a group calling itself "Team Viper" to blow up seven buildings in Phoenix, Arizona in an attempt to disrupt the government through the creation of chaos and fear. Inspection of their arsenal of weapons found two machine guns, fifty six boxes of 11,463 rounds of ammunition, six rifles, two pistols, fuses, blasting caps, and grenades along with hundreds of pounds of sodium nitrate and nitromethane for use as bomb-making materials (Brooke, 1996, p.1).
- **Nationalist terrorism**—These terrorists promote minority religious or ethnic interests and wish to be independent of majority rule, often driven by a desire to form their own government. Siegel (2003) mentions the assassination of India's prime minister, Indira Ghandi, in November 1984, by Sikh radicals trying to reclaim the homeland they believed was stolen by the government. Her murder was in retaliation for the government's assault on their revolutionary base the previous June.
- **Cause-based terrorism**—Terrorists of this type promote violence to attract followers to a particular religious or social cause. Although we immediately think of Osama bin Laden and his followers, Bartol (2002) reminds us of the doomsday cult called the Supreme Truth Sect. In 1995, followers of the cult released sarin nerve gas into the subway system in Tokyo, Japan; their attack killed eleven people outright and injured over 5000. Siegel (2003) cites radical anti-abortion groups that attack doctors and bomb abortion clinics as another example of cause-based terrorism.
- **Environmental terrorism**—Terrorism of this kind is designed to stop what some view as harm to animals (as in setting lab rats free) or harm to the environment through unrestricted building and development. Such domestic terrorists identify themselves as environmentalists and one particular group, the Earth Liberation Front or ELF, was extremely active during the 1990's. Members set fire to a new

ski resort in Vail, Colorado that they claimed was intruding into animal habitats. The arson caused an estimated $12 million dollars in damage (Siegel, 2003).

Revenge is a motivator for acts of domestic terrorism as is a strong sense of righteousness related to the behavior. Some theorists posit that terrorists are emotionally disturbed individuals with self-destructive urges and impaired upbringing (Jurgensmeyer, 2000). It is easy to imagine that the mind of a terrorist is irrational at best and psychotic at worst however, terrorism is often a rational strategy undertaken to achieve an objective (Barkan & Snowden, 2001).

Interrogation Strategies for Police and Fire Investigators

Revenge firesetters are individuals bent on achieving what they regard as justified and positive ends to some perceived wrong. An essential element found in the interview of the revenge arsonists we have assessed is that they feel victimized by someone or something with resultant anger and resentment. A significant number of revenge firesetters, by self-report history, claim that they were bullied in childhood and adolescence. Comprehensive research over the past twenty years has identified bullying in schools as a serious and common problem (Elliot, 1992; Wolff, 1999; Olweus, 1978). An interesting study of over 6000 Maltese students in multiple grades found that victims of bullying experienced feelings of anger, self-pity, and vengefulness while the bullies mainly felt either sorry or indifferent about their behavior. The study also determined that more male than female victims felt vengeful, and that more female than male bullies felt sorry for their conduct (Borg, 1998, Dec.). Although the comments that follow assume interaction between adult revenge arsonists and fire bombers, investigators, the dynamics described apply to youthful revenge setters as well.

The knowledge that a revenge arsonist may have experienced bullying in school is important as it relates to setting the stage for questioning. Such life experience may enhance feelings of suspicion and guardedness and a belief in getting even for perceived wrongs. Establishing a theme of "getting even" may resonate with the suspect and suggest that you understand and appreciate that way of thinking. Obtaining background about a past history of being a victim of bullying can be used by investigators to shape questions and decide upon an interrogation style.

As you determine the interrogation strategy, there are a number of factors about paranoid thinking worth remembering. Recall that revenge firesetters generally have a paranoid perspective on life, including a basic distrust of others. A person with paranoia does not generally engage in small talk and will not "warm up" during the process of the interview. Such an individual is easily angered and irritated and does not relate on an emotional level, so attempting to form an alliance, or conversely, assume a threatening style, does not generally work to your advantage. Additionally, someone with a paranoid thinking style lacks humor, so "joking around" is never a good ploy as it is misinterpreted. The suspect is a vigilant observer of others' behavior so pay attention to your own body language and verbal exchanges. Do not mirror the suspect's gestures or posture as some sort of indication that you are in tune with him. Someone who is paranoid is hypersensitive and may believe you are mocking or making fun of him. We recommend a neutral tone and a non-threatening posture and attitude.

We recognize that most investigators have had some training in body language (kinesics), but we wish to add a number of points related to interviewing in general and specifically to the interview of revenge firesetters and fire bombers. As mentioned above, your own body language is of utmost importance when interviewing someone with a paranoid thinking style who is alert to your every nuance. Be careful not to turn away from the suspect, as it can be interpreted as disrespect, or sit back with your arms folded across your chest as you may give the impression of boredom. Although those ploys may, and do, work with many individuals, they generally are not successful with paranoid thinkers.

Eye contact is regarded as a significant factor in the interview process and investigators are often taught to attach importance to how direct a person's gaze is during questioning. It is vital to remember that when a person is paranoid and mistrustful of others, his gaze is not steady on you and he certainly does not invite you to look closely at him. Lack of direct eye contact may not be an indication of guilt or anxiety but rather is self-protective. Additionally, as investigators, it is important to understand the cultural background of the suspect. Some cultures, such as Asian, believe that direct eye contact is rude and disrespectful and may not make eye contact as a sign of respect, not guilt.

Sapp et al. (1994) determined, and the Center for Arson Research supports the finding, that the revenge arsonist sets an average of thirty-five fires before a first fire arrest. This knowledge allows the interrogator to conjecture that the suspect has secrets and a vested interest in keeping them. Strategically, it also allows you to recognize that the individual is not a novice at the crime or any emotions connected with it. You are aware that revenge firesetters have a tendency to think in a paranoid way and will be alert for any signs of trickery or deceit on your part. Recognition of the suspect's thinking style and probable skill as an arsonist should be considered as elements of your strategy.

Place the interview chairs so the suspect does not feel crowded. Do not touch a subject with paranoid thinking unless it is unavoidable; your touch may be misinterpreted as aggressive or sexual in nature. We do not recommend showing photos of victims of arson or bombings you think may be the suspect's responsibility. Generally, such a technique is called upon to elicit an emotional reaction, such as guilt, or a physical reaction, such as turning away, from the sight. A physical reaction in someone who uses paranoid thinking may reflect internal stimuli more related to the impression that you are attempting a trick than as any response to the photos. Additionally, victims and property damage are intended by the offender and are hardly likely to cause the shock or horror you may be trying to elicit.

Finally, anticipate that a suspect with paranoid thinking may attempt to challenge your self-esteem by making derogatory remarks about you. Resist all attempts on your part to humiliate the suspect in return. Keep your eye squarely on the primary goal of the session, which is to obtain a confession.

Chapter 6

Thrill Seeker Firesetters

Anthony was a very interesting and important man in his community. He seemed to have everything a man could ever want: a wife (his fifth), two sons he saw occasionally (second wife), a nice house, and an exciting career as an insurance investigator specializing in arson fraud. He was a civic leader and spoke eloquently at fund raisers, especially for the local police and fire departments. Tony had always been interested in police work and actually tried to join a big city police department years ago, but failed the psychological. The testing psychologist wrote, "This applicant is cunning and manipulative and suffers from shallow affect and a complete lack of empathy. He is prone to boredom and devoid of guilt. I strongly recommend against hiring him to the department. He is a smoking gun." Tony got over the disappointment, although he always believed that the psychologist "screwed me over because I wasn't a typical 'yes' man, just telling him what he wanted to hear." Tony was extremely successful in his job as an investigator and often found proof of arson when even seasoned police and other fire investigators failed. He testified frequently in courts as an arson expert and helped his company save millions of dollars in denied claims. Tony was also partially responsible for putting three people in prison for arson despite their claims of innocence and lack of direct evidence. Everybody in the community respected him. No one could guess that Tony was a man of many secrets. Starting when he was about eleven, Tony set fires and discovered he was good at it. He especially enjoyed experimenting with timing devices and remote ignition switches as he got older. By the time he was twenty, Tony estimated he set over a hundred fires and, at his current age of forty-nine, he believes he set over 500 fires, many to occupied homes and businesses. He is responsible for many of the fires his insurance company has

89

him investigate and he was the arsonist for the three fires that sent innocent people to jail. He believes himself to be brilliant, a man among men, and much smarter than any of the police and fire investigators working arson cases. After all, they have no clue about him.

Thrill seeker firesetters are defined, for the purpose of the text, as those individuals who set fires as a way to experience danger and the sensation of risk. Such arsonists enjoy the risk of setting fires and the powerful idea of "getting away with" a crime. Arson is a validation of their intellectual superiority over other individuals, other men, in particular. Some research identifies the attraction to risk as a component of temperament evident early in life (Zuckerman, 1991). Temperament seems to be inherited and does not appear to be based upon parents' attitudes or other variables, such as gender or social class (Thomas & Chess, 1984). Other research supports the idea that risky behavior is an attitudinal response developed sometime after childhood (Jessor & Jessor, 1977). Table 6.1 compares demographics between thrill seekers (10 percent of the total population) and all other firesetters studied for the purposes of this text. As is observed in the other subtypes, the preponderance of firesetting behavior is largely male with white males over-represented in the thrill seeker subtype.

Zuckerman, Kolin, Price and Zoob (1964) developed a rating scale to define when optimal stimulation occurs in individuals. During a research study, they determined that some participants scored in the high range of sensation-seeking behavior. Those subjects appeared to become bored

Table 6.1
Comparison of Demographics between Thrill Seeker Firesetters and All Other Subtypes

Variable	Thrill Seeker Firesetters	All Other Subtypes
Female	9%	10%
Male	91%	90%
White	69%	48%
Black	28%	45%
Hispanic	3%	6%
Other	0%	1%

easily, conformed less to social rules, and were highly sensitive to inner sensations. Other studies found differences between males and females related to sensation- seeking behavior with males scoring significantly higher than females (Ball, Farnill & Wangerman, 1984; Zuckerman & Neeb, 1980).

Other social scientists have studied risk proneness as a predictor of risky sexual behavior, particularly in adolescents. Researchers have determined a relationship between sensation- seeking and teen-age high-risk behavior (Zuckerman, 1991; Block, Block & Keys, 1988). Zuckerman (1991) found that adolescents who scored high on the sensation-seeking scale he developed also were more likely to have more sexual partners and sexual experiences than their peers who had low sensation seeking scores. Adolescents with risky sexualized behavior seem less likely to have good self-regulation skills, according to Feldman & Weinberger (1994). To that end, youth with poor self-regulation skills appear to engage in problem behaviors, including substance abuse, poor school performance and an inability to delay gratification (Wulfert, Block, Santa Ana, Rodriquez & Colsman, 2002).

Youth with poor self-regulation skills may be deficient in key developmental accomplishments found in the middle years of childhood, the time between the ages of seven to twelve years. Minuchin (1977) stated that certain developmental assumptions may be made about those middle years. The first is that individuals grow within a social context and that a child's developmental progress depends on the values and societal attitudes of the people with whom he lives.

The second assumption is that personality development is continuous and interconnected and that the middle years are a bridge between childhood and adolescence. Although temperament appears to be heritable, exposure to differing attitudes and expectations seem to influence personality development in youth (Thomas & Chess, 1984). Theorists seem to agree that the emergence of self-regulation occurs by the middle years and is the result of interactions between personal characteristics and the environment (Bronson, 2000). Minuchin's (1977) third assumption is that change and growth occurs unevenly and uniquely in each child.

During the middle years of childhood, there is a focus on social, cognitive, and individual development. In this important stage of growth, children develop self-esteem, a self-concept, and an understanding of their social-sexual roles. Minuchin determined that successful completion of the tasks of the middle years are necessary for movement into the tasks of adolescence. Egan and Cowan (1979) identified particular tasks that children must accomplish during the years of seven to twelve, including cooperation with peers and others, becoming adept at basic relationships, learning to accept feedback about themselves from others, and skill development. During this phase, children identify themselves as industrious and capable or inferior and incapable, leading to poor self-esteem and feelings of inadequacy.

Two moral developmental theorists, Jean Piaget and Lawrence Kohlberg, proposed that children cannot learn moral reasoning until they have some degree of cognitive maturity, something that occurs during the middle years of childhood. Piaget (1932) posited that children develop moral reasoning in two stages. Stage one, called the morality of constraint, characterizes the reasoning of young children as being simple and rigid because they are learning the concept of rules. In this stage, children are certain of what rules mean and think concretely in terms of black and white. Stage two, called the morality of cooperation, is the time during which children learn that moral standards are flexible and can be changed. In this late childhood stage, children develop logical thinking skills and the ability to solve problems.

Papalia and Olds (1995) observe that in the late stage of childhood, youth are learning to look for the intent behind a behavior and think that the punishment should fit the crime. Minuchin (1977) posited that such consideration of intent taught problem-solving skills by allowing the consideration of various aspects of an issue.

By comparison, Kohlberg (1969) proposed that there are three levels of moral reasoning development. The first he termed pre-conventional morality (ages four to ten), during which time children obey rules to avoid punishment and gain rewards. During level two, called conventional morality, children, ages ten through thirteen, obey rules to please others and maintain order. In level three, called post-conventional morality, youth, age thirteen or older, have internalized the ideals and concepts of morality. Kohlberg's theory about the development of moral reasoning is not without critics, however. Gilligan (1982) noted that Kohlberg's theory stressed "masculine" virtues, such as justice and fairness and de-emphasized "feminine" values, such as caring for others.

Some individuals appear to lack the ability to reason through the prism of morality. These individuals, commonly called psychopaths, create heartbreak and destruction for people whose lives they affect. In this chapter, we explain the basis for our theory that thrill seeker arsonists have psychopathic personalities.

What is a Psychopath and How Do Psychopaths Develop?

On the face of it, and at the explanation's most basic descriptive level, psychopaths are those individuals who are unable to experience the feelings of love, sympathy (feelings for), and empathy (feelings about) for other people.

By way of review, Freud (1946), in his seminal work on understanding human behavior, conceptualized that there were three main structures to behavior. The first, called the *id*, Freud posited as an internal structure, present at birth, that stores all biologically-based aggressive and sexual drives. Freud believed the id was the unconscious source of psychic energy, drives, and instincts and that it operated on the pleasure principle: the seeking of immediate gratification. Freud maintained that the id represented the motivation of all human behaviors.

The second structure, called the *ego*, houses the rational decision making center and serves to filter id drives into socially-acceptable conduct. Ego development, which begins to develop in the first year of life, filters drives from the id into socially-acceptable behaviors. It is during this phase that children learn that some behaviors are rewarded while others are punished. The primary job of the ego, which operates under the reality principle, according to Papalia & Olds (1995), is to find realistic ways to satisfy id drives even while delaying gratification. The ego, like the id, has no concept of right or wrong and, therefore, is not responsible for moral choices (Santrock, 1995).

The ability to regulate emotions and delay gratification is identified as ego control in some developmental studies. Along with ego control, the concept of ego resilience (an ability to adapt to environmental demands) appears to relate to self-regulation around one's emotions and behavior. The capacity for ego control and ego resilience is in place by the middle years of childhood (Koop, 1982; Bronson, 2000). Children who do not learn self-regulatory behavior by the middle years seem at risk for problem behaviors, such as substance abuse, sexual risk-taking, and school under-performance (Wulfert, et al., 2002).

The third structure, called the super-ego, develops about the age of six. It is responsible for moral choices and understands the difference between right and wrong. The super-ego includes the conscience and exists, in part, at the level of conscious awareness (Santrock, 1995). Developed through association and identification with important and powerful authority figures (parents), the *super-ego* identifies behavior that is punishable and, therefore, negative, as well as behavior that is rewarded and is, therefore, positive. It is during latency (the middle years between seven to twelve) that children learn to channel their drives into socially-rewarded behaviors.

During the pivotal middle years of childhood, children further their development of the social behaviors and attitudes they will use throughout their lives. The age group between seven through twelve imitate what they see and experience from the important adults in their world. Schools and teachers play a significant role in the development of self esteem and positive social roles.

Historically, American schools were important in teaching children right from wrong. Until the mid-nineteenth century, morality was traditionally taught in public schools. The tone was non-sectarian in nature, but strongly reflected protestant ideology, expressed through bible reading and prayer. By the end of the nineteenth century, public schools developed a purely secular format that emphasized teamwork and the virtues of honesty, tolerance, and kindness. During the 1960s, the theory of teaching morality to children was strongly influenced by John Dewey who thought that children learned moral lessons best through reflective thought rather than formal readings (Panel on Moral Education, May, 1988).

Table 6.2 compares variables related to positive behaviors and attitudes in thrill seeker firesetters and all other subtypes. On the face of self-reported behavior, the thrill seeker firesetters in the study appear to engage in more acts of self destruction and delinquency, as well as more sexual activity and substance abuse than all other firesetters as a cohort.

It is essential that children have a caring adult to teach them the virtues desired in our society. Initial positive experiences in infancy and toddlerhood teach children that they are loved unconditionally and that the world is a safe place. These first experiences teach young children the concept of trust, according to Unell & Wyekoff (1995), necessary for learning moral values and virtues. Albert Bandura (1977) a leading proponent of social learning theory,

Table 6.2
Variables Related to Attitudes and Behaviors by Percentage

Variable	Thrill Seeker Firesetters	All Other Subtypes
Impulsivity	88%	86%
Behavior Problems	47%	58%
Chronic Lies	88%	81%
Theft	66%	57%
Problems with Authority	39%	34%
Sexually Active	53%	28%
Remorse for Behavior	31%	20%
Substance Abuse	50%	27%
Juvenile Justice History	53%	34%
Self-Abuse (banging head, punching walls)	54%	24%

posited that we learn how to behave by watching the behavior of others important to us. Santrock (1995) believes that we learn how to treat others and learn how to feel about things by observing the important people in our lives.

The middle years of childhood also involves learning how to use a sense of humor to address the conflicts, problems, and pleasures that come from interacting with others, at home, and elsewhere. Jokes of this age group reflect impulse-ridden fantasies and peer-group interactions. Humor enables children to negotiate through difficult times by teaching them how to laugh at themselves. Children in the middle years use humor to deal with unexpected social situations that cause them anxiety and make them feel unprepared (Gesell & Ilg, 1946).

During the middle years, children expand their self-understanding to incorporate other people's perceptions, expectations, and needs. They develop behavioral standards, learn more about how society works, and develop a belief that they can manage their own behavior according to social and personal standards (Papalia & Olds, 1995). Of interest is the observation that individuals diagnosed as psychopaths fail in the ability to understand others. Cleckley (1976) noted that psychopaths are selfish and ego-centered, unable to truly consider another's needs. Feasibly, it appears that psychopaths somehow do not learn the lessons of the middle years necessary to function as productive members of society.

Learning how to feel about people and situations is instrumental in the development of emotional expression. Lazarus (1991) has studied the development of emotions and their expression for decades. Lazurus contends that each emotion has an attendant appraisal process which allows the individual to decide whether the relationship between him and the emotion is harmful or beneficial. Table 6.3 describes the emotion and the accompanying relational definition of the emotional state, according to Lazarus.

Table 6.3
Relational Themes and Core Emotions

Emotion	Theme
Anger	An offense against me or someone important to me.
Anxiety	An uncertain existential threat.
Fright	An immediate, concrete, physical threat.
Guilt	Transgression of a moral imperative.
Shame	Failure to live up to an ego ideal.
Sadness	The experience of an irrevocable loss.
Envy	Wanting what someone else has.
Jealousy	Resenting a third party who seems to threaten the loss of another's affections.
Disgust	Being too close to something unacceptable.
Happiness	Making progress towards a realized goal.
Pride	Enhancement of ego identity through taking credit for a personal achievement for the achievement of others with whom we identify ourselves.
Relief	The departure or change for the better of a goal-distressing condition.
Hope	Wanting the best, but fearing the worst.
Love	Affection, either desired or in actuality.
Compassion	Feeling moved by another's suffering and wanting to help.

Note: Adapted from Lazarus (1991, p. 122).

It is fair to assume that the capacity to identify and understand one's own emotions and the feelings of others are essential tasks of the middle years of childhood. It is during the years between six through twelve that children internalize the standards society has set for them. As we will see, those individuals who grow up to assume the diagnosis of psychopathic personality do not develop the capacity to identify feelings, either in themselves or others.

There are also gender differences in the middle years, with girls appearing more socially poised by age ten and with a greater capacity to share intimate feelings and thoughts with their friends. Both boys and girls are receptive to social information and are open to learning prejudice or tolerance through the teaching of significant others. Children of this age forge friendships with their same-gender peers and those friendships serve to make them more sensitive and loving towards others. The practice of friendship teaches children to respect and value the opinion of others (Gisell & Ilg, 1946).

There are important lessons that are learned in the years between childhood and adolescence that have tremendous implications for socialization skills throughout life. Children who do not learn those skills find themselves in social disharmony from their early years. Lee & Robbins (1995) note that lack of positive development, along with a poorly realized sense of belonging, produce children who have problems identifying with peer groups in the middle years. As adolescents, they struggle with shallow relationships or seem drawn to deviant asocial groups. Berry (1993) notes that it is during the middle years that children learn to place themselves into the shoes of another through the ability to identify with other people. This ability is lost to those individuals who suffer from psychopathy, as we shall explore more fully in this chapter.

Asocial delinquent conduct that begins in the middle years of childhood seems to relate to higher rates of serious crime over a longer period of time in both genders. Tolan & Thomas (1995) suggest that the behavior and social attitudes of children under age twelve should be considered as predictive of future criminality. The time between age seven to twelve is when children learn to reason deductively and to play by the rules. A study by Leonard & Decker (1994) posits that a positive relationship exists between unacceptable behavior and a lack of attachment and commitment to others and society's values. When the lessons associated with the middle years are not learned, all too often society pays the price.

Before we move on in this chapter, it seems important to define our terms more completely. There is some confusion about the difference between a psychopath, a sociopath, and someone with an antisocial personality, and today, these terms are used almost interchangeably. Bartol (1999) points out that the use of the term psychopath has always been controversial. In the early nineteenth century, Philip Pinel, a French psychiatrist, described a certain pattern of behavior which manifested itself in remorselessness and complete lack of restraint as insanity without delirium. Bartol mentions that in 1888, a German psychiatrist, J. Koch, identified a constellation of behaviors as arising from what he called a psychopathic inferiority that he believed were related to genetic flaws. People with these genetic flaws were basically evil and unable to resist wrong-doing. Our modern day understanding of psychopathy leans heavily on Koch's perception of the behavior.

Over time, other theorists developed their own understanding of psychopathic behavior and in 1930, G.E. Partridge proposed that individuals with psychopathic behavior were created, not born, and he re-termed such maladaptive behavior as sociopathic, not psychopathic. Because there was so much confusion about what diagnostic label to apply, the American Psychiatric Association (APA) decided in 1952 to abandon use of the term psychopath and adopt the term sociopath in the *Diagnostic and Statistical Manual* (DSM), the official handbook of the psychiatric community.

Such change did little to stem the confusion, however, and in 1968, the APA changed the diagnosis from sociopath to personality disorder, antisocial, and the *DSM* manuals published in 1980, 1987 and 1994 continued to use antisocial personality disorder as the diagnostic term to specify certain behaviors and attitudes. Individuals with antisocial personality disorder must meet certain criteria, according to the diagnostic manual (the latest version-*DSM-IV*, 1994). Table 6.4 delineates the criteria for antisocial personality adapted from the *DSM-IV.* Readers are encouraged to review Table 6.2 to identify behaviors and attitudes of thrill seeker firesetters in the study.

A criticism of the antisocial personality criteria found in the *DSM-IV* is the focus on behavioral attributes without an equal emphasis on attitudes and emotions. The *DSM* does not indicate the emotional flatness found in such individuals, nor the self-centered, superficial charm found

Table 6.4
DSM-IV Criteria for Oppositional Defiant Disorder

I. Disregard for the rights of others since age fifteen, with at least three of the following:

- impulsive,
- manipulative, conning others and lying,
- behaves in a way that provides grounds for arrest,
- aggressive,
- irresponsible,
- lack of remorese.

II. Age eighteen or older.

III. History of childhood conduct disorder.

IV. Antisocial behavior is not a product of a psychotic episode.

Note: From the *Diagnostic and Statistical Manual*, 1994, p. 650.

in many with the diagnosis. Curra (2000) points out that the terms antisocial personality disorder, psychopath, and sociopath are ambiguous and represent an ongoing attempt to explain why some apparently normal people can do really terrible things. Further discussion in this chapter underscores the writer's belief that thrill seeker arsonists fit the profile of the psychopath (the term I favor). They have not learned the important and vital lessons of the middle years of childhood leaving them unable to empathize or sympathize with their victims.

In 1982, an experienced psychiatrist, Hervey Cleckley, developed a clinical checklist of the patterns and characteristics of the psychopath, based upon his years of treating them in his practice. Cleckley's list followed his seminal work on the psychopath called *The Mask of Sanity*, first published in 1941 which described the personality traits of the psychopath, including glib superficial charm, shrewd intelligence, and a lack of personal values. Cleckley, perhaps best remembered for co-writing *The Three Faces of Eve*, was concerned that psychopaths used their skill to avoid responsibility for their behavior, including persuading judges that they were mentally ill and, therefore, in need of treatment, not prison. A publication entitled, "Antisocial Personality-Part 1" (*Harvard Mental Health Letter*, Dec. 2000) describes the prototype psychopath as probably male, with a total indifference to others who manipulates by intimidation, deception, or both. Table 6.5 describes Cleckley's Checklist for Psychopathy.

Bartol & Bartol (2005) make the point that individuals who have antisocial personality disorders engage in a pattern of disregard for, and violation of, the rights of others, beginning in early childhood. Because they are so little affected by the impact their behavior and attitudes have on people, they are perfectly placed to become persistent criminals. Attempts at understanding the mind of a true psychopath have been an ongoing clinical challenge. Articles on the nature of psychopathy began to appear in scientific journals during the 1930s and continue to this day. It is difficult to really comprehend how someone could appear perfectly normal and charming in every way and yet could be purposefully harmful to others for his own amusement or for some other personal goal. This observation is of importance to any student of firesetting behavior, as certain of the subtypes, particularly the thrill seeker; seem to set fires just to set them - to see if they can get away with it.

Table 6.5
Cleckley's Psychopathy Checklist

Key Features	Other Characteristics
☐ Manipulative	☐ Trivial Sex Life
☐ Superficial Charm	☐ Unreliable
☐ Above-Average Intelligence	☐ Untruthful
☐ Absence of Psychosis	☐ Failure to Follow a Life Plan
☐ Absence of Anxiety	☐ Suicide Attempts, Rarely Genuine
☐ Lack of Remorse	☐ Impulsive Antisocial Behavior
☐ Failure to Learn from Experience	
☐ Egocentric	
☐ Lack of Emotional Depth	

Note: Adopted from Cleckley, 1982.

According to Frazier & Carr (1964), psychopaths knowingly engage in amoral acts with a complete understanding of the possible consequences. They note that psychopaths feel little anxiety or regret; and if experienced, the emotions are transient and focus on the consequences to themselves, not their victims. McCord & McCord (1964) described psychopaths as unable to form any lasting emotional bonds to others. Psychopaths, according to Maxmen & Ward (1995), seem incapable of the most basic of human emotions, including shame, loyalty, and love. The authors mention that, although psychopaths are quick to anger, they do not even hold onto that emotion for any length of time. It is clear that psychopaths suffer from a lack of emotional depth that extends to all aspects of their lives. They seem to identify most often with the feelings of boredom, depression, and frustration. They can be easily persuaded (or persuade others) to engage in wrongful activity because they enjoy the excitement. Table 6.6 compares variables related to emotion in thrill seekers and all other firesetters. In each of the variables, thrill seeker arsonists self-report the mood-related variables at a higher percentage than the other subtypes.

Dr. Robert Hare, considered one of the world's leading experts on psychopathy, conducted his initial research on the behavior in the Canadian prison system. In 1970, Dr. Hare developed three categories to identify types of psychopaths: primary, secondary, and dyssocial. Of the three, he considered only those placed in the primary category as "true" psychopaths. According to Hare, primary psychopaths had distinguishing characteristics (as described in Table 6.4), while the other two categories made up much of the general criminal population. Secondary psychopaths commit violent

Table 6.6
Variables Related to Emotion by Percentage

Variable	Thrill Seeker Firesetters	All Other Subtypes
Mood Swings	41%	36%
Depression	50%	34%
Excessive Anger	69%	67%
Seeks Excitement	25%	12%
Easily Led	50%	42%

crimes because of severe mental problems while dyssocial psychopaths are individuals who model violent behavior learned from a subculture (Bartol & Bartol, 2005).

In the psychological testing Hare (1970) conducted on psychopaths, the subjects usually scored higher on intelligence testing than members of the general population. Hare (1993) consequently revealed that he became reluctant to administer psychological tests to psychopaths in prison as they often were quite knowledgeable about the instruments. Psychopathic offenders self-reported what they perceived would be of the most benefit to them. As a result, Hare and his students spent years perfecting the Psychopathology Checklist, universally accepted as a scientifically-sound instrument to aid in the diagnosis of the psychopathic personality.

Hare (1993) divided particular symptoms of psychopathy into two categories: emotional/interpersonal and social deviance. He described the egocentric emotional/interpersonal style of the psychopath as glib, superficial, deceitful and manipulative, devoid of empathy, remorse or guilt, and shallow emotional depth. From the perspective of social deviance, Hare noted that psychopaths are impulsive, have poorly functioning behavioral controls, a need for excitement, and evidence problem behavior from childhood.

Maxmen & Ward (1995) believe that any expression of guilt does not affect the future negative conduct of a psychopath and note that they crave stimulation as though it was a drug. Siegel (2004) mentions that criminal psychopaths continue their illegal behaviors long after other criminals burn out or change. Psychopaths who engage in crime run the gamut from passing bad checks to violent, sadistic murder. Bartol & Bartol (2005) describe psychopaths as lacking in excessive worry and anxiety and observe that they do not have the symptoms associated with any mental illness. The writers also observe that psychopaths cannot understand the feelings of love another person might have because their own feelings are superficial and shallow.

An article in the *Harvard Mental Health Letter* (2002, Feb.) cited a German study that found psychopaths do not respond normally to any emotional stimuli, pleasant or unpleasant. Additionally, the study (which involved watching a series of slides under controlled conditions) determined that psychopaths do not associate feelings with behaviors or images as others do. They are able, however, to respond with the appropriate words when asked to describe the scenes they were asked to view. One study found that psychopaths have a greatly reduced ability to feel fear and apprehension and, therefore, are not afraid to take risks or face punishment (Lykken, 1996).

Despite the observation that psychopaths do not have any discernible symptoms of a major mental illness, there does seem to be a relationship between psychopathy and a history of attention deficit disorder and aggression and impulsivity in childhood (Moffit, 1990; Loeber & Schmaling, 1985). Other research has found a strong relationship between psychopathy and substance abuse. Cleckley (1964) found that even small amounts of alcohol impacted on psychopaths in a dramatic way, making them loud, vulgar, and obnoxious. In fact, Cleckley believes that psychopaths who are alcoholics are not capable of insight and show not the slightest desire to change, even when their drinking has essentially destroyed their lives. An article in the *Harvard Mental Health Letter* (2000, Dec.) stated that many psychopaths are substance abusers with addictions that begin early in life, are long lasting, and treatment resistant. As with other negative consequences of their behavior, psychopaths seem generally untroubled about the impact addiction has on their lives. As reported in Table 6.1, 50 percent of the thrill seeker subjects identified themselves as active substance abusers in comparison to 27 percent of all other firesetters.

For those of us who come in contact with psychopaths, either through the process of arrest, legal representation, clinical evaluation and treatment, or in everyday life, we need no convincing of the psychopath's ability to deceive. The lack of connection between the individual's behavior and his recognition of its consequences on himself and others is baffling. His behavior appears to have no contextual meaning and his actions are always self-serving. Table 6.7 compares the feelings associated with setting fires by thrill seekers to all other firesetters. Thrill seekers in the study self-report a significant increase in feelings of power/excitement than do all others as well as increased levels of boredom and intrigue about setting fires along with a complete absence of remorse for their behavior. On interview, most of the thrill seekers in our population (including those not in this current study) do not bother to identify with an emotional state that might serve as some sort of an explanation for setting fires.

Table 6.7
Comparison of Feelings in Firesetting Behavior

Variable	Thrill Seeker Firesetters	All Other Subtypes
Anger	3%	9%
Depression	3%	5%
Fear/Anxiety	16%	20%
Power/Excitement	28%	0%
Happiness/Relief	6%	12%
Intrigued	9%	1%
Stupid	0%	1%
Remorse	0%	7%
Boredom	13%	8%
Emotion Unknown	25%	32%

Table 6.8
Comparison of Variables Related to Firesetting Behavior
by Percentage

Variable	Thrill Seeker Firesetters	All Other Subtypes
Anger	13%	25%
Revenge	0%	4%
Peer Influence	0%	6%
Fun	13%	7%
Boredom	38%	4%
Experimentation	9%	3%
Relief	0%	3%
Depression	0%	2%
Psychosis	0%	2%
Accidental	0%	3%
Motive Undisclosed	19%	27%
Attention	3%	3%
Denial of Behavior	3%	10%

Note: Accurate within < or > three percentage points.

The thrill seeker firesetters in the Center for Arson Research study generally demonstrate the attributes ascribed to psychopaths in the preceding paragraphs. Review and comparison between thrill seekers and all other firesetters on their motivations for setting deliberate fires reveal a number of interesting findings demonstrated in Table 6.8. Thrill seekers in the sample began their firesetting behavior around the age of eleven while the average for all others was age ten years. Again, motivation is self-serving and is offered on interview with no regard as to the impression he makes on the evaluator about his crimes.

Etiology of the Psychopath

The etiology of psychopathy is still not clearly understood although a number of factors appear to be involved. A predominant cultural bias in research literature presumes that poverty contributes greatly to antisocial behavior but a hard look at the poor demonstrates that most people living in poverty do not develop into psychopaths. Individuals with antisocial behavior also come from middle and upper class families and as Maxmen & Ward (1995) observe, the behavior of psychopaths in childhood is remarkably similar no matter what the socioeconomic status or social class of the family.

Research indicates that psychopaths grow up in homes where there is an over-abundance of chaos and parental discord. A number of social scientists have posited that antisocial behavior develops when the mother rejects her child or is inconsistent with affection or discipline (Glueck & Glueck, 1959). An earlier study by Knight in 1937 on severe alcoholics posited that those with psychopathy lived with domineering, but inconsistent, fathers and weak, indulgent mothers as children. Supporting Knight's earlier study, Robbins (1966) observed that psychopaths grew up in homes where the father was either an alcoholic or had an antisocial personality disorder. McCord & McCord (1964) concluded that neither the psychopathic child nor his or her parents love one another so no bonding can occur. Without bonding, identification between parent and child cannot take place which is necessary to produce anxiety of possible rejection by the parent for rule violation. However, as Maxmen & Ward (1995) point out, many psychopaths grow up in normal homes with loving parents.

Siegel (2004) notes that a number of studies found psychopaths have lower skin conduction levels than non-psychopaths, suggesting a link between antisocial behavior and the autonomic nervous system which controls physiological reaction to emotions. Psychopaths do seem to need a higher than normal level of excitement in their lives than is found in the general population. There has been some suggestion that psychopaths may have some degree of frontal lobe brain damage. This finding has some significance as the frontal lobe is instrumental in inhibiting antisocial behavior. Most research scientists would no doubt agree that there are most probably multiple causes for the development of psychopathy.

The Criminal Psychopath

Many psychopaths are not criminals and, in fact, often experience some degree of success in their chosen careers and their personal lives until they grow restless or behave impulsively. Many psychopaths display the behaviors attributed to the disorder without ever running afoul with the law, including chronic lying, manipulation, shallow relationships, and poor job performance. They suffer from extreme boredom and are cunning, selfish, and unreliable in their dealings with others. Because they lack a moral compass, psychopaths fail miserably at telling the truth and are unreliable and irresponsible. Psychopaths who are criminals have demonstrated evidence of antisocial behavior since childhood.

The question has been raised as to whether psychopaths are different from other criminals or if all criminals are psychopaths. A study by Kessler et. al. (1994) determined that 1.2 percent of females and 5.8 percent of males in the general population suffer from antisocial personality disorder, closely aligned with psychopathy. There is a group of individuals who persistently engage in antisocial behavior, featuring impulsivity, thrill seeking gratification, with multiple, diverse victims from childhood throughout adult life (Porter, 2000). This group, called criminal psychopaths, represents approximately 20 percent of the total prison population (male and female) according to Hare (1993).

One of the most chilling aspects of certain criminal psychopaths is found in their perception of sexual gratification. Cleckley (1964) described the sex lives of psychopaths as trivial and impersonal without any emotion other than the relief of immediate sexual tension. It is characteristic of adult thrill seeker arsonists to self-report multiple failed relationships with little (if any) regret. Interestingly, 53 percent of the thrill seekers in the study reported an active sex life while 28 percent of all other subtypes reported being sexually active. Yablonsky (1982) writing about the violent sexual patterns of sociopathic adolescent gangs noted that their attitudes about their female victims were ones of disdain and hostility. The following chapter on disordered coping firesetters more fully explores the association between criminal psychopaths and sexual violence.

A Closer Look at Two Thrill Seeker Arsonists

One of the better known thrill seeker arsonists within our recent history is Paul Keller, who set over 100 fires between 1992 and 1993 in the Seattle, Washington area. Mr. Keller was convicted of the three murders of elderly victims of a nursing home he set on fire. He pled guilty to thirty-two arson fires and admitted to forty-four additional fires (Norton, 1993). He was sentenced to ninety-nine years in prison and faces release in 2078. In childhood and adolescence, Paul Keller was considered a loner in school and caused trouble at home, but as an adult, he became a success in the family advertising business and appeared an upstanding member of his community. He was known to police and fire fighters as a supporter of their efforts and in fact, had tried several times to join the fire department, only to be turned down.

Mr. Keller claimed in his confession to the police that his firesetting began when he was twenty-seven and continued until he was arrested at age twenty-eight. According to the offender, he set fires to churches, nursing homes, warehouses, people's homes, and businesses. He was finally arrested after his father turned over evidence and shared the family's suspicions with the arson task force assigned to investigate the fires (Wurzer, 1995). Mr. Keller denied that he was a criminal and blamed his firesetting on alcoholism.

A second infamous thrill seeker arsonist, John Orr, was a well-known fire investigator in Glendale, CA who was ultimately sentenced to life in prison for killing four people trapped in a fire he set at a hardware store. After his arrest in 1991, Mr. Orr pled guilty to a total of six cases of arson although some fire investigators believe he was responsible for setting over 2,000 fires. The offender was subsequently featured in a book by author Joseph Wambaugh called *The Fire Lover* and in a special NOVA documentary entitled *Hunt for the Serial Arsonist*. Mr. Orr reveals his pathology in the documentary by appearing to lecture the viewing audience on the profile of the serial arsonist wanted for the very fires he was responsible for setting. It is only some time later that the viewer realizes that Mr. Orr is actually lecturing from behind prison bars.

In an amazing glimpse into his thinking style, Mr. Orr wrote a letter to one of the lead investigators responsible for bringing him to justice. In this letter (obtained from the Court TV website, www.courttv.com) dated May 11, 1992, Orr asks Captain Casey to cooperate with his own private investigator to "refute charges" against him. Another letter by Orr (www.courttv.com) dated October 21, 1992, was directed to the sentencing judge asking for consideration on sentencing. I urge any student of human behavior to review this remarkable document as it speaks volumes about the mind of a thrill seeker. In his letter, Mr. Orr asserts that he was personally responsible for the apprehension of hundreds of criminals when he was a security guard and that this training led to his career in fire investigation.

Mr. Orr denies setting the fires for which he has pled guilty and blames poor legal advice and representation on his plea bargain. He further blames Captain Casey (mentioned above) for mishandling the evidence (Orr's fingerprint on a piece of paper used as part of the incendiary device) and wonders if that paper was brought to the arson scene to purposefully implicate him. Mr. Orr next advances the idea that the US Attorney's Office had a personal vendetta against him and asks the sentencing judge for a new trial.

One of the more bizarre aspects of the case involved a manuscript written by Mr. Orr, discovered during the investigation, about a serial arsonist named Aaron who was a firefighter with no expectations of getting caught. Mr. Orr makes the case that his writing was misinterpreted as an indication of his guilt. In the NOVA documentary, Orr states that he "took literary license" to describe Aaron as a firefighter/firesetter who torches a hardware store, killing five. In the book, Aaron set fires on his way home from arson investigation conferences. At his trail, Orr pled guilty to setting fires on his way back from arson conferences.

One of the arguments Orr makes to the sentencing judge in his letter is that if he could be sentenced to probation for the crimes he did not commit, he could focus on working and a probable writing career to pay restitution. He goes on to say that if he were guilty, then he deserved clinical analysis, not the "one hour chat" with a psychologist prior to sentencing. He also notes that he is facing bankruptcy and that enforced confinement is a hardship on his family, who are suffering financially as a result of his imprisonment. In a final altruistic burst, Mr. Orr expresses his concerns for the prison officials who would be burdened by having to protect his safety if he were sentenced to incarceration because he was a well-known peace officer. He assured the judge that a sentence of home confinement would be more than enough punishment for an innocent man.

Firefighters as Firesetters

In 2003, the Federal Emergency Management Agency (FEMA) published a report entitled *Firefighter Arson* as part of their technical report series. The document underscores the scarcity of research into firesetting overall and by public safety personnel particularly. Accurate reporting by states on the number of arson fires, let alone arson fires set by firefighters, is generally unavailable. A number of states refuse to acknowledge that a problem exists but overall, the team gathered by FEMA posited that nationally, firefighters who set deliberate fires appear to be on an increase.

The team of experts who gathered to write the FEMA report determined that firefighter arsonists escalate the scope and number of their fires over time. They identified a primary motivation of this type of arsonist as the desire to be seen as a hero. While this may be a component of the dynamic, especially for the younger firefighters, investigators should be aware that a larger component of the motivation is for the thrill of getting away with the crime. In our experiences of interviewing firefighter arsonists (approximately twenty-five over the years), the idea of setting fires and then fighting them, surrounded by other unsuspecting men, was the prime motivation for the crime. Daring rescues, bringing out victims from burning buildings, administering CPR—all part of the thrill related to the risk of discovery.

Interrogation Strategies for Police and Fire Investigators

Thrill seeker arsonists are heavily invested in feeling "one up" on male investigators. It is important to keep in mind that they feel no guilt or remorse for their crimes so do not plan, as part of your strategy, to employ the use of photographs of victims or property destruction. Appealing to the better nature of the suspect also has little to recommend it, especially since the likelihood is that the individual may well be a psychopath and, as such, is interested only in himself.

It is absolutely essential to have an interrogation strategy well in hand before any attempts are made to question someone you have reason to believe is a thrill seeker arsonist. Understand that it is very important to establish the credibility of the investigation and the evidence in the suspect's mind. The arsonist is generally well aware of the paucity of direct evidence linking him to specific fires. He has the knowledge of how many fires he has successfully set over time and how skilled he has been at eluding detection. Unlike many other kinds of criminals, if the suspect is a psychopath, he is reading you at the same time you are reading him. Usually the strategy of redirecting the suspect's thoughts from the crime to the justification for the crime does not work with psychopaths. They already have myriad excuses for their conduct and will see your strategy for what it is—an attempt to get them to talk. It is important to recognize any preconceived notions you may hold about thrill seekers and work actively to rid yourself of them or at the very least, place them in your reserve file.

It is essential to gather as much background data on the suspect as you can before the interview. Remember that the thrill seeker arsonist is generally intelligent and adept at reading your signals. He waits to hear how much you know before he decides what to say. He is not burdened by a guilty conscience and does not need to get anything off his chest. He has no desire to form a bond with his interrogators, unless he believes it will work to his advantage. Sapp et. al. (1994), in their study of thrill seeker arsonists, found that the average age of onset for firesetting behavior in this subtype was twelve years while the Center for Arson Research found the average age for the subtype was eleven. The importance of the age of onset is that, as an investigator, if you are interrogating an adult suspect, you may be faced with an individual who has set many fires over a long period of time without detection. He, therefore, has every reason to feel confident in your presence.

The Sapp team further reduces thrill seeker arsonists into subtypes (excitement, attention, sexual, recognition) but, for the purposes of this text, we use the term thrill seeker to describe an individual who sets deliberate fires for the excitement of danger and to reinforce a sense of superiority over others. Although the Sapp team identified one individual who set fires for sexual excitement, we have not had that experience. The arsonists we have evaluated, who have a sexualized dynamic as a component of their motivation, we place in the subtype of disordered coping firesetters, discussed in the next chapter.

Thrill seeker arsonists, according to Sapp et al. (1994) enjoy setting big fires and return to the scene within twenty-four hours after the fire was set to survey the damage. Thrill seeker arsonists give no thought to getting caught and would set other fires, even if they believed themselves to be suspects. Our findings correspond to those of the Sapp team and we agree with their assessment that thrill seekers do not confide their behavior to anyone. They do not have a desire to interrupt their dangerous activity.

Sapp et al. determined a number of attributes they believe are specific to thrill seeker arsonists: white males with less than twelve years of education and above average intelligence. Such individuals may have a history of foster care, juvenile justice involvement, and a stable work history in adult life. Thrill seekers grow up in two-parent families and have warm relationships with their mothers and cold, distant relationships with their fathers. Our studies support the Sapp findings; in our current sample, only 3 percent report a history of foster care, however, while a full 59 percent had one or both parents missing from the home. Of the various subtype designates given by Sapp et al. to their study of thrill seeker arsonists, their identification of the excitement motivation arsonist most closely resembles the Center for Arson Research thrill seeker. The Center for Arson Research and the Sapp team both identify thrill seekers as responsible for setting multiple fires over the life span.

All background information that you can gather will be helpful in determining the interrogation strategy that has the best chance of success. A working assumption going into an interview with an adult thrill seeker arsonist is the presumption that the suspect is a psychopath. Therefore, your understanding of psychopathy will be of enormous benefit to you. Remember that psychopaths are glib liars and are adept at deceit and redirection. It is important to recognize that the suspect may know as much about the interpretation of body language as you do, so be aware that he may be purposefully arranging his posture to send you particular messages that may be at complete odds to his actual feelings. Although writers, such as Gilbert (1986) point out that a suspect with crossed arms, rigid posture, and poor eye contact is "obviously nervous", I urge you to suspend such absolutes in judgment about psychopaths.

If your department has skilled female investigators, I recommend that a female officer is often the best choice for interrogation of the thrill seeker. The game of superiority played by the thrill seeker is directed at other males and they are often insulted at being questioned by a woman. It has been our experience at the Center that adult thrill seekers tell more of the truth to our female evaluators for two compelling reasons: (1) because the superiority game is not played with women and, therefore, admissions of guilt do not count, and (2) because such admissions of guilt are thought to trigger the evaluator "getting the boss" to hear the confession, leading to a resumption of the game.

Remember that if the suspect is a psychopath, he will not have fear of the police or anxiety about the future. We advocate that your basic approach is neutral and that you do not allow your own feelings to become aroused by the suspect. If you have a female interrogator, she should have the choice seat with male officers appearing subordinate to her. Of all things you could design as strategy, that approach feels insulting to the thrill seeker and he finds it more difficult to resist showing off for the benefit of the male officers. Above all, do not become discouraged if your initial interrogation does not yield results. As Sapp et al. (1994) point out; thrill seekers are questioned on average five times before confessing.

Chapter 7

The Disordered Coping Firesetter

Paulie is a nine-year old boy with some big problems. By the time he was five, Paulie had been placed in eight foster homes where he lasted only a few months until his placement agency was called to take him away. In his longest stay, he had been sexually and physically abused by the nineteen-year old son of the house. Paulie had been removed at birth from his mother's care; she was thirteen at the time of delivery after becoming pregnant by an older cousin. In and out of foster care since birth, Paulie finally was placed with a good family who loved him and made the decision to adopt him. Since that time, the adoptive family's world has been turned upside down. Paulie has stolen from them, is openly defiant of rules and authority, engages in dangerous behavior, including hitchhiking, drinking, and smoking marijuana. He has been psychiatrically hospitalized three times, twice for serious aggression and once for a suicide attempt by running out into traffic. He has been on multiple medications to control his behavior, but is non-compliant with the regime.

At school, Paulie is constantly in trouble and has been expelled from two schools in his district this year. His female teachers are afraid of him because he becomes aggressive when he doesn't get his own way; in fact, he punched one of his teachers in her stomach. He is failing fourth grade because he generally won't do his work and, if he does any, he refuses to turn it in. He is in frequent fights with peers and blames them for his actions. He has no friends at school or in his neighborhood. Paulie refuses to accept responsibility for his behavior and does not seem to learn from mistakes.

In addition to his other behaviors, Paulie has a secret behavior that no one knew anything about until very recently. Whenever he gets upset, as soon as he can, he sets a fire. Paulie began setting fires when he was about four and a half and knows they are the only thing that makes him feel better. By his own estimate, Paulie has set over seventy-five fires of all sizes. In fact, the size of the fire never matters and he often stamps on or rubs out the flames. What is important to Paulie is striking that match and seeing something start to burn. He recognizes that he feels better immediately and describes fire, "As the only real thing that calms me down." Although fire used to be ideal for removing Paulie's anger, it doesn't seem to be working as well as it once did. Paulie feels increasing rage as he gets older and his fires are becoming more frequent. Last week, Paulie was caught starting a fire in the stairwell at school. The police were called and Paulie was taken out of school in handcuffs. His parents are at their wits' end; they had not been informed about his firesetting by the agency prior to his adoption.

Disordered coping firesetters are defined, for the purposes of this text, as those individuals who set fires in order to return to a state of emotional equilibrium after experiencing intense anxiety, rage or both. As we shall see in this chapter, disordered coping firesetters have many of the behaviors and attributes of the thrill seeker, including symptoms of psychopathy. There are a number of significant differences between the two subtypes (and all other subtypes), however, the most important of which is the motivation for a fire event.

The Center for Arson Research random sample determined that ninety firesetters (29 percent of the total sample population) fit within the parameters of the disordered coping subtype. The demographics of the subtype are found below in Table 7.1. Female firesetters are more evident in the disordered coping subtype than in the others and blacks are represented disproportionately to all others. As the reader will notice, the average age of the first firesetting evaluation is three years younger for the disordered coping subtype than for all others.

Disordered coping firesetters, in general, present a more compromised clinical picture than is found in the other subtypes. They appear to have more symptoms related to emotional dysfunction and poor connectedness to others than are identified in the other subtypes. We have found

Table 7.1
Comparison of Disordered Coping Firesetters
and All Other Subtypes

Attribute	Disordered Coping Firesetters	All Other Subtypes
Male	88%	91%
Female	12%	9%
White	41%	54%
Black	53%	38%
Hispanic	6%	6%
Other	0%	2%
Mean Age at First Firesetting Interview	12 years	15 years

that as they get older, disordered coping firesetters do not seek help from social supports (and in fact, seem not to expect help) and have very poor coping strategies for responding to moments of stress. As children, this subtype demonstrates serious problems in virtually every area that reinforce feelings of competence and self-worth. Table 7.2 compares variables related to problem areas in disordered coping firesetters and all other subtypes. It seems clear, from the sample and from the more comprehensive number of cases of disordered coping firesetters not included in this study, but known to the writer, that this subtype has great trouble self-regulating behavior and suffers from a failure to meet social expectations, standards and values. Simply stated, disordered coping firesetters seem to be in trouble everywhere and with everything starting at very young ages.

Violence, Abuse, and Neglect

Various studies have demonstrated that the earlier children are exposed to violence, abuse or neglect, the more likely it is that they will be become involved in acts of delinquency and adult criminal behavior (Widom & Maxfield, 2001; Ireland & Widom, 1995). Childhood maltreatment, including physical, emotional and sexual abuse, physical neglect, lack of proper adult supervision and educational and moral-legal maltreatment, have long-range ramifications (Kelley, Thornberry &

Table 7.2
Comparing Variables in Disordered Coping Firesetters
and All Other Subtypes

Variable	Disordered Coping Firesetters	All Other Subtypes
Hyperactivity	69%	57%
Poor Concentration	71%	63%
Learning Problems	66%	51%
Behavior Problems (home, school, community)	76%	49%
Impulsive Behavior	90%	84%
Lying	91%	76%
Excessive Anger	76%	63%
Stealing	67%	53%
Fighting	71%	62%
Friends	28%	61%

Smith, 1997, August). Other research by Schwartz, Rendon & Hsieh (1994, Sept.-Oct.) disputed the claim that maltreatment leads to delinquency and called for more research into the relationship. An earlier article by DiLalla and Gottesman (1991) theorized that the relationship between physical maltreatment and antisocial behavior in children might be overestimated. However, the preponderance of available research data appears to support a relationship between the two elements.

A number of studies (Trickett & Kuczynski, 1985; Main & George, 1985) have looked at the relationship between maltreatment in childhood and a capacity for empathy. The Main and George study on preschoolers determined that children with a history of physical abuse demonstrated either aggression or a complete lack of empathy towards other children in distress. A closer look at some applicable data suggests troubling factors related to behavior in the lives of disordered coping firesetters. From the results of the findings, it may be inferred that disordered coping firesetters have difficulty with self and social regulation skills to a greater degree, overall, than the other firesetting subtypes.

Table 7.3
Variables Reflective of Self-Regulating Skills

Variable	Disordered Coping Firesetters	All Other Subtypes
Animal Cruelty	22%	12%
Cruelty to Small Children	30%	13%
Property Destruction (excludes firesetting)	68%	57%
Self Abuse	32%	23%
Problems with Authority	42%	37%
Remorse for Behavior	19%	22%
Delinquency History	29%	39%
Mental Health History	46%	38%

An Overview of Violence

Chaiken (1998) observed that the most powerful demographic predictors of violent criminality are gender, race, and age. The Center for Arson Research considers deliberate arson to be an act of aggression, targeted directly or indirectly at others. It is clear from various studies cited earlier in this text (see review of the literature) and from our own work that males far outnumber female firesetters in all subtypes. Age of onset for setting fires seems to depend upon the subtype although, apart from accidental/curiosity firesetters, disordered coping youth have the earliest age of onset, at six years old, via their own recollections and supportive documentation. Minority males are disproportionately and consistently represented in the juvenile justice and adult justice systems, according to various studies (Bilchik, 1999, July; Blumstein, 2001, Feb.; Huizinga, D. & Elliott, D., 1987; Sealock & Simpson, 1998). Interestingly, they are also overrepresented in the disordered coping subtype (53 percent black) to 41 percent white) and are underrepresented in the revenge and thrill seeking subtypes (see Chapters 5 and 6).

There are additional factors related to violent behavior beyond age and gender. A detailed study on factors related to juvenile delinquency and adult criminality, sponsored by the National Institute of Justice, found that abuse and neglect in childhood increased the probability of antisocial conduct by 29 percent (Widom & Maxfield, 2001, Feb.). Another study by Kelley et al. (1997, Aug.) sampled 1,000 youth identified as high risk for delinquency, their caretakers, and various records over the course of a number of years from middle through high school. The research determined that 14 percent of the sample had maltreatment histories and 86 percent did not. The study also determined that there were significant differences in the social class and family structure of youth identified as maltreated.

In reviewing data, it is important to recognize that research often fails to control for social class. Minorities are frequently over-represented for two reasons: unconscious bias during the assessment process and the greater poverty found in minority families overall. For instance, a number of studies determined that African-American children were more likely than white youth to suffer serous injury or death from maltreatment (Hampton, 1987). However, a survey under-taken by Gallup in 1994 determined that 12 percent of white respondents, but only 9 percent of black respondents revealed that they had been punched, kicked, or choked by an adult when they were children (Maguire & Pastore, 1995).

Review of a number of additional variables found in the experiences that disordered coping firesetters report, or recalled, having, as children, reinforced their exposure to factors related to violence, abuse, and neglect in their youth. Readers are reminded that the Center does not collect direct data related to socioeconomics of the clients seen for evaluation or consultation. Interestingly, except for the variable of absent father, disordered coping firesetters generally score significantly higher than all other combined subtypes. Of note, all subtypes reported the same degree (29 percent) of witnessing domestic violence within their homes. We did not collect specific data on neglect although neglect was frequently mentioned in supportive documentation.

The study by Main and George (1985) targeted children living in poverty, many of whom came from one-parent families existing on welfare. Half of the targeted group had histories of maltreatment and half did not. Main and George observed that the children who had no history of maltreatment, but lived in poverty, demonstrated kind, pro-social behavior to other children who were distressed about something. They concluded that the stresses themselves experienced by economically-struggling families did not impact negatively on their children unless there was also maltreatment

Table 7.4
**Factors Related to Delinquent/Asocial and Criminal Behavior,
Comparison by Percentage in Disordered Coping Firesetters
and All Other Subtypes**

Variable	Disordered Coping Firesetters	All Other Subtypes
Family Discord	81%	74%
Domestic Violence (as a witness)	29%	29%
Absent Mother	14%	6%
Absent Father	32%	43%
Both Parents Absent	34%	15%
Foster Care	38%	10%
Residential Placement	40%	31%
Physical Abuse (reported)	36%	24%
Sexual Abuse (reported)	17%	6%
Emotional Abuse	21%	13%

Note: Self-reports of abuse were verified through records and other source documentation made available to the Center for Research staff.

involved. However, earlier research by Gil, (1970); Pelton, (1979) and Giovannano and Billingsley (1970) found a strong relationship between the stresses of poverty and child maltreatment.

A study by Hampton and Newberger (1985) determined that hospitals report the highest numbers of child maltreatment cases, most of them related to physical abuse. They also posited that reports were filed based upon the unconscious bias of the medical treatment staff. Hampton and Newberger identified several factors that influenced the decision to report abuse: the race of the abuser (blacks and hispanics reported more often than whites), physical abuse was reported more often than any other type of maltreatment, and people earning less than $25,000 per year were reported more often than those earning more than $25,000.00 per year. Statistics available on the rate of child abuse and neglect cases in the United States vary widely and there is no main, absolute data source that allows us to be certain about the number of youth who suffer from maltreatment each year. Cases of child abuse and neglect by upper and middle class families are thought to be reported less often because they simply do not come to the attention of authorities. A maltreated child, seen by a private physician is sometimes unreported especially if the doctor is an acquaintance of the family. A study conducted in 1985 found a 47 percent reduction in reported abuse but members of the scientific and treatment communities credited the study more with optimism than accuracy (Gelles & Strauss, 1987, June).

Data from a 1995 survey determined that the rate of substantiated abuse and neglect cases was more than 1 million per year. Of that number, approximately half of the youth suffered from neglect, 14 percent were sexually abused, and 24 percent were physically abused while about 7 percent were neglected medically or emotionally mistreated (U.S Department of Health and Human Services). In a 2001 report, the National Child Abuse and Neglect Data System (NCANDS) found that slightly fewer than one million children had confirmed victimization from abuse or neglect (approximately 12.4 of every 1,000 children from birth to age seventeen). Their victimization included neglect in 59.2 percent of the cases; physical abuse in 18.6 percent of the cases; sexual abuse in 9.6 percent of the cases and emotional abuse in 6.8 percent of the cases. Some youth experienced more than one type of abuse. During 2001, an estimated 1,300 children died from abuse and neglect (U.S. Department of Health and Human Services, 2003). A review of Table 7.3 indicated that firesetters self-report levels of abuse at higher rates than the rates in the above report, except for the self-report of sexual abuse found in "all others" at 6 percent.

It may be impossible to know with great accuracy what the actual prevalence of child abuse is because we must rely on statistics from reports with an understanding that not all child maltreatment is reported. However, what data are reported present a chilling perspective of a national snapshot of abuse and neglect. The U.S. Department of Health and Human Services report (2003) indicates that child protective service agencies (the primary source of the data) received 2,673, 000 reports in 2001 of possible maltreatment of children and youth.

According to Bergman, Larsen and Mueller (1986) more than 90 percent of all child abuse occurs within the home. Bartol and Bartol (2005) determined that the highest victimization rates were of children ages three and under and that 87 percent of the victims of maltreatment were abused by one or both parents (p. 303). Libbey and Bybee (1979) observed that the average age of abuse in childhood was around five although adolescents also suffered from maltreatment. It appears that age and gender are important variables as they relate to abuse. Boys under twelve years are more likely to be physically abused than girls while girls over twelve are more likely to suffer abuse than boys. Girls are twice as likely to be sexually abused as boys (U.S. Department of Health and Human Services, 1995). Neglect seems to decrease as the age of the child increases, presumably because the youth is more able to attend to his own basic needs.

A number of studies point to neglect as possibly the most significant of all types of abuse in the lives of children. Widom (1989) studied the arrest rates of adult offenders convicted of violent crimes who had histories of abuse, neglect or both as children. He determined that individuals with a history of sexual abuse were slightly less likely than those without a history of sexual abuse to commit a violent crime. Offenders with a physical abuse history were slightly more likely to commit a crime of violence while those with a history of neglect were the most likely to commit a violent crime in adulthood. A study by Patterson, DeBaryshe and Ramsey (1989) identified two pathways for the development of adult criminal behavior: early starters who experienced coercive parenting as children and demonstrated antisocial behavior in childhood and late starters, who received inadequate monitoring by parents and demonstrated oppositional behavior in adolescence.

Monteleone (1994) noted that neglect hurts children in mind, body and spirit. He believes that neglect influences the developmental pathways of childhood, altering the steps from one critical phase of development to another. Smith and Thornberry (1995) found a relationship between abuse, neglect, and violence according to adolescent self-report studies. It seems clear that children exposed to abuse and neglect suffer from its emotional, physical and cognitive effects in school, at home, and at play (Emery, 1989; Haskett & Kistner, 1991). A study on youth violence conducted in Milwaukee determined that of twenty-nine juvenile homicide offenders, 45 percent reported living with serious domestic violence while 90 percent lived in single family homes (Rose, H.M., Maggiore, A. & Schaefer, B., 1998).

Physical Child Abuse and Neglect Models

There are a number of theoretical models that have been used to explain the cause of child abuse and neglect, but the problem is now accepted as much more complex than previously recognized. The descriptions that follow are not inclusive of all theoretical models, a discussion beyond the intent of this chapter. The first theoretical explanation for child maltreatment, the mental illness model developed during the 1960s, focused on the dynamics of the parents who abused their children. Gelles (1987) remarked that the psychiatric community has spent time and effort attempting to develop a profile of parents who were prone to child maltreatment. For instance, Glueck and Glueck (1959) and Rutter (1981) posited that sociopaths did not receive enough love or consistent discipline when they were children from their mothers.

The mental illness model proposes that parents who mistreat a child must have a serious major mental health problem, such as a psychosis. A study by Estroff et al. (1984) in a child psychiatric clinic compared mothers who maltreated their children to non-abusing mothers and found that the abusive mothers had more psychiatric symptoms and lower intelligence scores than the non-abusive control group. Earlier research reinforced the view that parents with specific types of emotional problems, such as psychosis or inadequate or passive-aggressive personality disorders, were at considerable risk for what was termed uncontrolled battering of children. Other abusers, called controlled batterers, were described as cold disciplinarians who had compulsive personalities (Boisvert, 1972). However, research has consistently demonstrated that no more than 5 percent of parental child abusers are psychotic (Johnson 1993; Justice & Justice, 1976). The mental illness model has largely fallen out of favor, but it represents an attempt to explain behavior that began to receive increasing attention by the public during the socially-chaotic decade of the 1960s.

A second theory, the social-psychological model, proposed that child maltreatment required three variables: a special parent, a special child, and stress (Helfer & Kempe, 1972). Stress, according to the model, may be acute or chronic and is identified by the parent as present within the family according to Campbell & Humphreys (1993) who noted that Helfer and Kempe did not address the significance of culture on child maltreatment. Campbell and Humphries also observed that other research has failed to support the notion that "special" children (with a physical or mental handicap) are more abused than non-special children.

Sociological models have emphasized the relationship between the environment, stress, and maltreatment of children. Child abuse appears more common in families where poverty is a key source of stress (Wauchope & Straus, 1990; Kruttschnitt, McLeod & Dornfeld, 1994). As Johnson (1993) mentions, the struggle to survive robs the family of dignity and drains it of energy, leaving frustration and anger in its wake. Some parents with inadequate or failed coping mechanisms lash out at the nearest available target, the child, as a method of stress reduction (Morse, Hyde, Newberger & Reed, 1977). However, as Campbell and Humphries (1993) note, the majority of parents living highly stress-filled lives do not abuse or neglect their children.

About Abuse and the Abuser

There appears to be no simple answer to the reasons that certain parents and perhaps certain kinds of parents maltreat their children. There is also recognition that adults, other than the parents, may be responsible for child maltreatment. Information gathered by the National Child Abuse and Neglect Data System (NCANDS) for 2001 demonstrates that although the abusers were most often parents (80.9 percent of the time, 15.9 percent of the abusers were babysitters, extended family members, and other caregivers). Approximately 3.2 percent of the identities of the perpetrators were unknown or unavailable. The NCANDS data for 2001 reveals that approximately 12.4 of every 1,000 children up to age seventeen were the victims of maltreatment in 2001. Interestingly enough, females were most often the identified abusers at 59.3 percent compared to 40.9 percent for males (NCANDS, 2003). This finding may be a reflection of the traditional role of women bringing them into more frequent contact with children rather than an indictment of the female psyche. A more recent study by Wauchope and Straus (1990) failed to identify significant gender differences related to the abuser.

Data from the NCANDS study (2003) determined that 48 percent of the victims of maltreatment were male while 51.5 percent were female and 0.5 percent was unknown to the study. Approximately 75 percent of the victims of maltreatment were age twelve and under. The survey by NCANDS also found that about half of all victims (50.2 percent) were white, 25 percent were African American and 14.5 percent of all maltreatment victims were Hispanic while American Indians, Alaskan Natives, and Asian-Pacific Islanders made up the other 3.3 percent of reported victims.

Research into the characteristics of those who neglect or abuse children indicates that generally they are angry and unhappy adults filled with stress and a lack of control over their own lives (Trickett & Susman 1988; Morse, Hyde, Newberger & Reed, 1977; Egan, 1983; Gil, 1979). Wolfner and Gelles (1993) observe that child abusers come from all walks of life and cannot be characterized by demographics such as age or educational level. Our experiences with firesetters allow us to concur with the findings that abuse is not restricted to a particular social class, education, or economics. A number of studies posit that adults who were themselves victims of abuse are, in turn, more likely to abuse their own children, thereby creating a cycle of violence (Campbell & Humphries, 1993; Trickett & Susmann, 1988; Egeland, 1993).

National interest into the problems of child abuse did not really flourish until the early to mid 1960s when publications began to focus on the plight of the battered child. The 1970s and 1980s brought attention to the issues of battered wives and, by a natural expansion, to the broader problem of family violence in the United States. Wolfe (1985) found that polls taken about the perception of the seriousness of child abuse by the general public ranked the problem at 10 percent in 1976 and at slightly over 90 percent in 1983.

The World Health Organization (WHO) issued a report in 2000 that identified the physical and sexual abuse of children and youth as an international problem. According to the WHO document, approximately 57,000 youth under the age of fifteen were murdered as a consequence of abuse with children four and under, representing almost double the death rate of victims above four. The WHO report clearly stated that many more children and youth suffer non-fatal abuse and neglect. By comparison, in 2000, the organization, Prevent Child Abuse America, conducted a national survey of all fifty states and determined that an estimated 1,356 children died as a consequence of abuse or and neglect.

Sexual Abuse

Sexual abuse which encompasses the exploitation of a child by a person for gratification or control (Whitcomb, 2001) often produces damaging and long lasting consequences for its victims. NCANDS ascertained that an estimated 9.6 percent of all reported abuse and neglect cases in 2001 involved sexual abuse. Females are twice as likely as males to be victims of sexual abuse, according to the U.S. Department of Public Health (1995). However, it is important to remember that many victims of sexual assault delay reporting, do not ever report, or are too young to report, their victimization, so the true incidence of sexual abuse is unknown (Erez & Tontodonato, 1989).

Increased reporting of sexual abuse, however, provides us with a more accurate picture of the prevalence rates of sexual abuse than we had in the past. NCANDS used their 2001 data to determine that there are nearly 1.2 child victims of sexual abuse for every 1,000 youth under the age of eighteen, which translates to 86,830 victims in 2001. A survey by Epstein and Bottoms (1998) of 1,712 college students found a 17 percent occurrence rate of sexual abuse before age eighteen. An earlier survey of women in the San Francisco area disclosed that 38 percent of the respondents reported intra- or extra-familial sexual abuse by the time they turned eighteen (Russell, 1983). As noted in Table 7.3, 17 percent of the disordered coping subtype and 6.0 percent of all other firesetter subtypes reported a history of sexual abuse (supported in other documentation).

The sequelae of sexual abuse are many and varied. Although some victims may cope adequately with their abuse, others suffer from chronic psychological and behavioral problems, such as heightened fear and anxiety, post traumatic stress, sexualized behavior, and poor self-esteem (Gelles & Conte, 1990, Nov.; Siegel, 2004). Some child abuse victims become youthful sexual abuse perpetrators against others, generally those younger, smaller, and weaker. It should be mentioned, however, that not all victims become assailants as children, or in adulthood, although a history of sexual abuse does increase the potential for other antisocial behavior (Widom, 1995, March).

Monteleone (1994) identified a number of risk factors that point to potential sexual abuse victims in childhood. The risk factors include: females, children, particularly between ages eight-twelve, disruption in the family system, including parental absence and parental discord and a nonbiological father present in the home. Monteleone and others, (Trickett, Aber, Carlson & Cicchetti, 1991; Elmer, 1977), also described factors related to child abuse in general, such as: poor parenting skills, an unwanted child, lack of parental bonding, overwhelming stress, and a lack of social supports, poverty, substance abuse, domestic violence, unreasonable expectations of children, and the acceptance of corporal punishment as the primary discipline.

The Impact of Abuse

The often devastating results of the maltreatment of children increase the potentiality of delinquency by 50 percent and adult criminality by 38 percent to those who were its victims, according to Widom (2000). Her study also revealed that subjects with a history of maltreatment were significantly more likely than subjects without a history to attempt suicide. They were also more likely to meet the criteria for antisocial personality disorder. In an earlier study, Widom (1995) found that people who were victimized sexually as children were at a higher risk for arrest as adults for committing crimes, including sex crimes, than people who did not suffer from maltreatment as children. However, the risk for arrest in adulthood was no greater for childhood victims of sexual abuse than for physical abuse or neglect. Widom also determined that the vast majority of childhood sexual abuse victims had no history of criminality as adults.

Children who are victims of maltreatment are subject to long-lasting physical and psychological harm as a result of abuse and neglect (Reid, 1997; Aber & Allen, 1987) with residuals that may well be overlooked by treatment and justice professionals. Head and brain injuries may result in impairment of neurological and intellectual functioning, with a direct impact on learning readiness and development and speech delays (Kendall-Tackett, Williams & Finkelhor, 1993; Monteleone, 1994). Children with a history of abuse also suffer from problems with attachment, behavior, and discipline, as well as aggression and low self-esteem (Oates, Forrest & Peacock, 1985; Haskett & Kistner, 1991).

There are many other recognized sequelae and behavioral indicators associated with child abuse, including, but not limited to, withdrawal, anxiety, runaway and delinquent behaviors, inhibition, hyper-sexuality, behavioral extremes, such as over and under compliance and conduct disordered behavior (Lutzker, Bigelow, Swenson, Doctor & Kessler, 1999; Einbender & Friedrich, 1989; Heindl, Krall, Salus, & Broadhurst, 1979). It is generally recognized that for many victims, the effects of abuse and neglect are serious and last well into adult life.

Application of Maltreatment to Disordered Coping Firesetters

Our experience with the disordered coping subtype suggests to us that many of the clients we have interviewed suffer from the manifestations of maltreatment and that those behavioral and attitudinal symptoms last well into adulthood. In fact, because we have entered our twentieth year as an agency, we have the experience of re-interviewing clients we first saw as children who have continued to set fires as adults. For many, fire continues to offer comfort and stress reduction, while other substitute behaviors seem to provide less adequate relief. In other words, despite a variety of learned intervention strategies, for many of the subjects, in moments of stress, anxiety, or anger, firesetting remains the coping strategy of choice. Table 7.5 reviews firesetting motivation for disordered coping firesetters and compares it to the motivations found in all other firesetting subtypes.

There are a number of general observations that may be made about the list of motivations in Table 7.5. It is important to understand that motives are not suggested to the interviewee by the evaluator, but rather are supplied by the client during the assessment process. One thing that has remained a constant discovery for our staff is that disordered coping firesetters almost never deny setting fires, unlike the other subtypes, where denial of firesetting is not particularly uncommon, especially in the

Table 7.5
Comparison of Motivations for Setting Fires by Percentage

Motivation	Disordered Coping Firesetters	All Other Subtypes
Anger	38%	17%
Revenge	1%	5%
Impress Peers	2%	11%
Fun	1%	10%
Boredom	4%	8%
Curiosity	3%	4%
Relief	9%	0%
Sadness	3%	1%
Hallucinations	1%	2%
Money	0%	0.5%
Crime Concealment	0%	0.9%
Refused to Discuss/ Did Not Know Motive	36%	24%
Deny Setting Fires	1%	13%
Emulate Movie Plot	0%	0.5%
Accident	0%	3%

delinquent subtype, at the beginning of the interview process. Although conjecture could be offered about the reasons leading to lack of denial, such as that firesetting has become a normalized behavior, we do not feel that we have adequately explored it enough to be certain. At the least, it is an interesting dynamic. Additionally, what remains clear is that anger and relief are the leading expressed motivations for setting fires while 36 percent claim not to know why they set fires. Typically, the denial of understanding the reasons for setting fires manifests itself most often with older adolescent and adult clients.

In addition to differences in the motives for setting fires, disordered coping firesetters offer differences in the number of fires they admit to starting, by the time of their interview, along with other factors, such as firesetting as a planned or spontaneous act and as a solitary or peer-related activity. Table 7.6 examines those findings. Differences between disordered coping and all other firesetters are their most profound in the percentage of disordered coping firesetters who have set more than ten fires at the time of the first evaluation as well as in the number who reported setting fires as a solitary activity. As a reminder to the reader, the mean age of the disordered coping client at the time of his interview was twelve years while the mean age of all other subjects was fifteen years. The mean age for the first episode of firesetting in the disordered coping subtype was six while it was eleven for all others.

Table 7.6
Comparison in Number of Fires Set and Other Related Factors

Variable	Disordered Coping Firesetters	All Other Subtypes
No Fires	1%	0.5%
One-Five Fires	41%	63%
Six-Nine Fires	6%	4%
Ten or more Fires	48%	20%
Set Alone	66%	34%
Set with Others	7%	36%
Alone and with Others	20%	19%
Fires were Planned	17%	19%

We are also interested in the origin of the idea to set fires as there are certainly many other behaviors a person could turn to in moments of stress and anxiety. A key question for those of us at the Center for Arson Research has always been 'Why fire?' and we continue to explore that conceptually. Certainly, matches and lighters are easy to find, so convenience may be one factor, but we do not think that convenience is the sole, or most significant, reason for firesetting. Table 7.7 examines client-offered reasons for the onset of their firesetting behavior. There are two findings that leap to the eye from our perspective: the disordered coping subtype seems significantly less influenced by peers and siblings than the other subtypes in the study and across all subtypes, there appears a general lack of awareness about how or why firesetting actually began as a behavior of choice.

The Center for Arson Research also collects data on the emotions the client associates with the firesetting event. From the perspective of utility, if a behavior is not rewarding, it is generally soon extinguished. It is reasonable then to assume that those who repeatedly set fires are finding some reward in doing so. Because the firesetting behavior in the disordered coping subtype is largely secret until the events are plentiful enough to permit discovery or significant enough to cause danger, it may be assumed that the reward is generally not that of gaining attention. Is it a possibility that the reward lies within the feeling state experienced by the

Table 7.7
Comparison of Original Ideas for Setting Fires across Subtypes

Variable	Disordered Coping Firesetters	All Other Subtypes
Client's Own Idea	10%	9%
Peer/Sibling Idea	3%	22%
Media	4%	4%
Hallucinations	1%	3%
Watching Fires	3%	2%
Parent/Other Adult	3%	1%
Uncertain about Origin	68%	47%
Refused to Discuss	8%	12%

Table 7.8
Comparing Feelings at the Act of Firesetting

Variable	Disordered Coping Firesetters	All Other Subtypes
Anger	11%	8%
Sadness/Depression	8%	4%
Anxiety/Fear	13%	22%
Power/Excitement	2%	4%
Shock	0.5%	0%
Happy/Relieved	26%	6%
Intrigued	1%	3%
Stupid	0.9%	1%
Confused	0%	5%
Remorse	1%	6%
Blames Others	3%	1%
No Feelings	9%	9%
Refused to Reveal or Uncertain about Feelings	30%	31%

Note: When subjects reveal more than one feeling, all are recorded.

firesetter? Table 7.8 compares reported feelings in disordered coping firesetters and all others. Seemingly, within the sample, disordered coping firesetters experienced more anger, depression, and relief at the time of their fires than did the other subtypes. We recognize that this paints a picture with very broad brush strokes and encourages more questions around the relationship between fire and emotion.

Generally, the youth we see in the disordered coping subtype carry one of three, or some combination thereof, diagnoses: Attention Deficit Hyperactive Disorder (ADHD), Oppositional Defiant Disorder (ODD), or Conduct Disorder (CD), while adult offenders most often carry an antisocial diagnosis (see Chapter 6 for a behavioral description). A brief review follows on the primary characteristics of each diagnosis. For a more comprehensive review of each diagnosis, please consult the *Diagnostic and Statistical Manual of Mental Disorders-IV*.

Table 7.9
Behavioral Characteristics of Conduct Disorder

- Persistent failure to comply with rules and expectations.
- Excessive fighting and intimidation with violence directed at people and animals.
- Property destruction.
- Robbery and theft.
- School truancy and suspensions.
- Failure to consider the consequences of behavior accompanied by risk-taking for its own sake.
- Conflict with authority figures at home, school and community.
- Chronic lying and deception.
- Failure to accept responsibility for behavior with a pattern of blaming others.
- Lack of remorse accompanied by insensitivity to the thoughts and feelings of others.
- Multiple sexual partners with superficial emotional engagement.

Table 7.10
Behavioral Characteristics of Oppositional Defiant Disorder

- Negativistic, hostile and defiant behavior.
- Acting as if authority figures are enemies with constant arguments.
- Temper tantrums.
- Defying reasonable rules and requests.
- Deliberate annoyance of others.
- Blaming others for mistakes and behaviors.
- Frequently spiteful and vindictive.
- Significant impairment in social, occupational or academic functioning due to behavior.

A careful review of Table 7.2 reveals that generally, disordered coping firesetters self-report behavior problems associated with ADHD, ODD, and CD proportionately more often than all other subtypes combined. Their behavioral histories, self-reported and substantiated through other documentation, support the presence of many of the symptoms found in

Table 7.11
Behavioral Characteristics of Attention Deficit Hyperactive Disorder

- Short attention span and problems attending with easy distractibility.
- Poor listening skills.
- Frequently disruptive, aggressive and negative attention-seeking activities.
- Blames others for actions and does not easily learn from mistakes or consequences.
- Hyperactivity with high energy, restlessness, loud, excessive talking.
- Impulsive with poor turn-taking skills and difficulty waiting.
- Poor self-esteem and compromised social skills.
- Forgetful, inattentive to detail and generally poorly organized.

the three primary diagnoses. A preponderance of the clients interviewed by the Center for Arson Research appear to reinforce the legacy of abuse and neglect through dangerous, negative, and inappropriate behavior.

In fact, studies demonstrate that youth who were maltreated have a higher rate of conduct disorder diagnosis and greater rule non-compliance than do youth without a history of abuse and neglect (Ammerman, Cassisi, Hersen & Van Hasselt, 1986). A study by Smith and Thornberry (1995) demonstrated that youth who were victims of maltreatment tended to behave more violently than youth without a history of abuse and neglect. There have also been studies that show the impact of removal from home and disruptions in the relationship with parents have a profound effect on future violence in children. Research, such as a London study by Farrington (1989), showed a relationship between violence in boys and separation from their parents before the age of ten. By way of reminder, 38 percent of the disordered coping subtype reported foster care placements while 34 percent reported the complete absence of both parents from their lives. Parental absence was accounted for by three primary reasons: the death of both parents, the abandonment by both parents, or the relinquishment, voluntary or involuntary, of parental rights.

The Concept of Resilience
Of great research interest to us is our recognition that the motivations which influenced the decisions to set fires as children essentially remain the motivations in adulthood, particularly in the revenge, thrill seeker, and

disordered coping subtypes. The links between maladaptive behaviors acquired in childhood and continued inadequate methods of coping appear particularly strong in the disordered coping firesetter. In childhood, adolescence, and adult life, firesetters in this group seem to lack the quality called resilience, defined for our purposes as the ability to bounce back from traumatic and burdensome life circumstances.

Some children appear to have certain characteristics of temperament and personality that allow them to weather even the toughest storms (Anthony & Koupernik, 1974; Garmezy, 1983; Murphy & Moriarity, 1976). Exposure to traumatic events or deprivation produces different responses depending on the age of the youth. Davidson and Smith (1990) report that children who initially experience trauma under the age of eleven are three times more likely to develop psychiatric symptoms than do youth who face initial trauma as adolescents. Research by Murphy and Moriarity found that there were some preschool-age children who managed to develop the ability to maintain a sense of personal integrity even in the face of great stress.

Although stress is a common feature of childhood, some youth are exposed, either as victims or witnesses, to enormous adversity beyond normal societal pressures. Of those children, certain of them appear to possess factors in their personalities that serve to protect them and afford them resiliency. Murphy and Moriarity (1976) called these children "good copers" with healthy narcissism. According to Papalia and Olds (1995, pp. 335, 336), the factors that help children cope successfully in the face of enormous challenges include:

- **Personality make-up**—Children who are resilient are positive thinkers and are friendly, sensitive towards others, and independent. They tend to feel competent and have good self-esteem. Such children feel connected to others and have a sense of mastery over their emotions (Block & Block, 1980).
- **Family**—Resilient children either have supportive parents or some other supportive adult who is interested in them and whom they trust.
- **Learning experiences**—Good copers tend to learn from watching others contend with bad or frustrating problems. They also have worked out solutions for themselves that worked and increase the feeling of competence.

- **Reduced risk**—Resilience seems to depend, in part, on children not having to contend with multiple stressors simultaneously.
- **Compensating experiences**—Other venues for positive rewards, such as a supportive educational environment, appear to provide support for children who have high-stress home lives.
- **Access to resources**—Good health, educational opportunity, as well as social services and supports also contribute to resiliency in children, according to Mrazek and Mrazek (1987).

The Absence of Resilience and the Presence of Risk

Just as we know that some youth recover from stress and trauma, we also know there are others who do not seem to have the capacity for bouncing back from adversity. Some children have lives that are comprised of multiple risk factors that strongly influence their emotional health. Rutter (1987) found that two or more risk factors such as poverty, a disturbed mother, or foster placement, placed a child at a fourfold risk for an emotional disturbance at some point in his life. The problems suffered by children without the requisite coping skills that help them bounce back often manifest themselves through negative behavior. A history of victimization serves as a catalyst for acting out behavior, including acts of violence in youth and adult criminality (Haskett & Kistner, 1991; Dodge, Bates & Pettit, 1990). Table 7.12 reviews a number of factors that place a youth at risk.

Readers are reminded that among the risk factors predictive of future violence are: aggression, family discord, substance abuse, family involvement in the criminal justice system, foster placement, poor school performance, and a lack of goals. The above-mentioned factors are by no means an exhaustive list, but rather are representative of the elements associated with risk for violence. Generally speaking, disordered coping firesetters appear to suffer to a greater degree from the risk factors associated with violence, although firesetters from all other subtypes appear to have those risk factors present to some degree. Readers are invited to see previous chapters for a review of the factors related to risk for violence in each of the subtypes.

Children who suffer from maltreatment and other risks associated with delinquency and adult criminality seem to share a breakdown, for whatever the reason, in the relationship between child and adult caregiver. Research

Table 7.12
Comparison of Risk Factors among Disorder Coping Firesetters and All Other Subtypes

Factor	Disordered Coping Firesetters	All Other Subtypes
Fighting	71%	62%
Fighting with Weapons (sticks, rocks, knives, guns, etc.)	12%	5%
Animal Cruelty	22%	12%
Cruelty towards Others (smaller, weaker, younger)	30%	13%
Family Discord	81%	74%
Substance Abuse (self)	21%	33%
Substance Abuse (parent)	46%	35%
Future Goals	33%	42%
Parent in Prison (one or both at time of interview)	7%	8%
Foster Care	14%	6%
Learning Problems	66%	51%

has found an association between the lack of parent-child communication, a high rate of family discord, low parental interest in the youth's life, and the presence of violent behavior in adolescence (Farrington, 1989; Elliott, 1994). A study found that 59 percent of violent youth were arrested again as adults and of that group, 42 percent committed a crime of violence associated with the offense (Hamparian, Davis, Jacobson & McGraw, 1985). An interesting study by Robins (1966) determined that males with a history of antisocial conduct between the ages of six to seventeen were more often charged with violent crimes, such as rape, murder, and other sex crimes, than were females with a similar history of early antisocial conduct.

Sex Offender Behavior and Arson: The Presence of Fantasy

Although a lengthy discussion of sex crimes is beyond the intent and scope of this text, the evaluators at the Center for Arson Research have found a decided trend in the sexualized fantasies and behaviors of disordered coping firesetters. We have collected self-report data on the presence of fantasies that may precede, accompany, or follow an act of firesetting for many years as one of the factors related to the study of motivation. Over the next several years, we intend to more closely sharpen our focus around the variable of fantasy as a result of our general findings. Non-scientifically stated, and offered as a point of discussion, we have found that fantasy does play a part in firesetting behavior across the subtypes, from the primitive and unsophisticated fantasies of small children, to the elaborate and well-crafted fantasies of adult arsonists.

Among the findings related specifically to disordered coping firesetters, we have noticed the self-reported presence of hostile and aggressive fantasies starting at a young age. Such fantasies appear to precede an act of firesetting, seem to center around the child's mother, and relate to making her "feel sorry" for something. We have not found the same sort of fantasy in the other subtypes, although revenge firesetters also have aggression-filled fantasies that appear to focus on "getting even" with someone for some real or imagined infraction. We have not found that the firesetter's mother is featured in these fantasies as a general rule. Instead, revenge fantasies seem outward directed against someone or something viewed as noxious to the subject.

As the disordered coping firesetter matures and passes through latency, the fantasies appear to shift away from mother to other female figures, perhaps known or unknown to the firesetter. With the onset of sexual maturity, the fantasies also shift from a generalized aggression to sexual aggression. The presence of such fantasies appears highly stimulating and is accompanied by masturbation, followed by an act of firesetting. Self-reports from recently reviewed records of adolescent and adult male disordered coping firesetters (approximately 150 clients in the sample) indicate that the act of setting a fire serves to release them from an acknowledged anxiety around the sexually aggressive fantasy and the rage associated with the fantasy. Unfortunately, we have also had multiple occasions to interview adolescent and adult offenders for whom the act of firesetting did not reduce anxiety or rage. It appears that the failed fantasy/firesetting sometimes reinforces sexual aggression, which upon occasion, is acted out through sexual assault.

An Overview of Sex Offenders with Adult Female Victims

It is difficult to arrive at an accurate estimate of the incidence of sex crimes because of the method of measurement and the definition of the reported offense. For example, sexual battery, for our purposes defined as intentional and wrongful physical contact without a person's consent and with a sexual component or purpose, is not reported in the Uniform Crime Reports (UCR). This is of significance because it effectively excludes the number of sexual assaults against males by males, a crime that cannot be classified as rape according to the UCR. Rape is defined as "the carnal knowledge of a female by a male forcibly and against her will" (FBI, UCR, 1999).

Although there is great fear of sexual assault among members of the general public, the incidence of the offense is less today than twenty years ago, according to Maletzsky (1991). According to UCR data, approximately 90,000 rapes or attempted rapes were reported to the police in 1991 (UCR, p. 29). However, the National Crime Victimization Survey (NCVS) estimated that in 2001, 248,000 rapes and attempted rapes took place, suggesting that the crime is significantly under-reported (Rennison, 2002). Forcible rape is the least reported of all violent crimes with the estimate that only one of every four is reported to the police (Schmalleger, 2002). Still, the NCVS also notes that the incidence of rape has fallen over the past several decades.

While there are separate theories, intervention strategies, and treatment modalities that surround the sex offender, some social scientists posit that sex offenders commit other crimes, as well (Weinrott & Saylor, 1991; Bench, Kramer & Erikson, 1997). This raises the possibility that sex offenders may be less "specialized" criminals than generally believed. The findings, based on longitudinal studies of identified sex offenders, have found important similarities between sex offender and non-sex offender criminals, including antisocial behavior and social isolation. Among the differences between sex and non-sex offenders, a study of rapists by Groth and Birnbaum (1979) found that rapists generally lacked close emotional relationships and committed rape for reasons of power and anger rather than for sex. Sex offenders are also more likely to recidivate with a sex crime than a non-sex crime offender and to recidivate frequently (Bonta & Hanson, 1995; Quinsey, Harris, Rice & Lalumiere, 1993).

There is recognition that a particular type of sex offender, the psychopathic offender, presents a great challenge clinically and in the criminal justice system. There appears to be a high prevalence rate for psychopathy among convicted rapists (Prentsky & Knight, 1991). The presence of psychopathy, along with other variables such as drug abuse and an unstable, antisocial lifestyle in the profiles of sex offenders are considered factors deserving of more study.

Disordered Coping Firesetters and Deviant Fantasies

Deviant sexual fantasies have become a recent and important area of research exploration. A number of studies recognize the importance of attitudinal distortion related to sexual arousal and deviance (Hanson, Gizzarelli & Scott, 1994; Abel, Becker, Blanchard & Djenderedjian, 1978). Laws and Marshall (1990) studied the relationship between fantasy, imagination, and overt sexual aggression in adult sex offenders. Aggressive fantasies are greatly important in motivating sexually deviant conduct, particularly in men convicted of rape (Abel, Becker, Blanchard & Guild, 1977). Other research has reinforced an association between sexual deviance, attitudes about women, and deviant sexual fantasies (Knight, Prentky & Cerce, 1994).

The results of our evaluations on disordered coping firesetters have increased our understanding about the function of deviant and aggressive sexual fantasies in this population. We recognize that the fantasies are masturbatory once the youth enters adolescence and tend to become elaborate and increasingly sexually sadistic as the individual matures. The fantasies provide a rich source of eroticized pleasure and also offer relief from sexual tension. Masturbatory activity in disordered coping firesetters is, by self-reports, ritualized. Firesetters in the subtype frequently have a locked room specific for the purpose of fantasy and masturbation. According to their own accounts, the room contains the impedimenta of deviant fantasies, such as pornographic videos, magazines, whips, and other articles associated with sadistic erotica. After an increase in sexual tension, these subjects describe locking themselves in the room, engaging in fantasy, and masturbating to orgasm.

The clients sometimes describe setting a small ritualized fire in a container specific to that purpose, after orgasm, as mentioned in a preceding paragraph. The fire appears to play an integral part in the behavioral complex and signals the end of the event. The firesetter seems to judge his lessening of tension around the effects of the fire, not the masturbation. In some way, not yet clear to us, the fire apparently offers the individual an understanding that the sadistic fantasy is ended. If the fire fails to decrease tension, this population reports the possibility of finding an innocent victim or a prostitute for sadistic sexual assault. If this should be the case, males who report the behavior describe setting another small, ritualized fire, which serves to reduce the anxiety and the cycle seems to end for that moment in time.

An Account of a Disordered Coping Firesetter

A number of years ago, I received a call from two homicide detectives who wanted advice on an interrogation strategy for a man they suspected of vicious sexual assaults, one resulting in death, on prostitutes in their community. The detectives provided the background that this individual, a forty-five-year-old white male, had been known to them over the years for various criminal events, including stalking and harassment of a number of women in the community. He generally worked as a night maintenance man in various apartment high rises, leaving jobs frequently, usually after evidence of firesetting in isolated locations in the buildings, such as in boiler rooms. The individual had never been charged with the crime of arson, but it seemed curious that he was the common element at various fire events.

According to the detectives, they conducted a background investigation on the suspect at the last apartment building where he had worked until a fire was discovered in the maintenance shop, when he quit. As the detectives went door-to-door, they asked the apartment dwellers if they had ever had any interaction with the maintenance man. People either said they had never seen him or that, if they needed any service, he responded promptly, attended to the problem and left. Those who had the occasion to meet him, described the suspect as "very quiet".

At one of the apartments, the detectives asked the woman who answered the door if she knew the suspect and she replied that she did because he had written her obscene letters for the past year. Quite surprised, the detectives asked her how she knew the letters were from him and if she had ever reported this to the police and she replied that she knew the letters were sent by the suspect because he signed his name.

She also said she had not called the police because they were very busy and she hadn't wanted to bother them. The detectives responded that the police were there to help the public and mentioned that receiving obscene letters must have been upsetting. She replied, "You bet they're upsetting. They're almost impossible to read!" With that, she told them to wait at the door and re-entered her apartment. Returning in a moment, the tenant carried a shoe box, tied with a ribbon, and opened the box. Inside were several dozen letters, still in their envelopes. Reaching in at random, the woman extracted a letter and opening it, showed the detectives what she meant-every word in the letter was written backwards. As the detectives tried to make sense of what they were seeing, the tenant stated, "Now you see what I'm talking about? The damn things are impossible to read! I have to hold them up to a mirror to see what he wants to do to me this week!"

Shaking their heads (the tenant refused to press charges), the detectives went on to a number of the neighborhood bars. They knew that the suspect had a reputation for drinking fairly heavily and that he had been involved in a few fights at a number of the local watering holes over the years but nothing major. They interviewed a number of bartenders, showing them the suspect's picture and asked if the bartenders recognized the man. The bartenders confirmed that they knew him, that he came in one or two nights an week, generally caused no trouble, had a few beers, and left.

At one of the bars, however, when they inquired information of that bartender, he said, "Oh yeah, I know him. He comes in two nights a week, regular as clockwork with his doll." The detectives were excited because this was the first concrete information they received associating him with a particular woman. They asked, "Do you know her name?" The bartender, puzzled, replied, "Whose name?" The detectives responded, "The doll's name." The bartender, looking at the officers as if they were unhinged, responded by saying, "What are you talking about?" and went on to describe how the suspect came in every week with a life-sized inflatable love doll.

According to the bartender, the suspect would carry in his doll and place her carefully at a high backed bar stool. He would then walk away and immediately return, lean over the doll, and ask if he could buy her a drink. He would nod the doll's head up and down and order two glasses of top-shelf scotch. For the next twenty minutes or so, the man would talk at the doll, occasionally holding a glass up to her latex lips. At the end of the twenty minutes, he would place a $20.00 bill on the bar, pick his doll up and carry her out.

The detectives, who went from incredulity to laughter during this account, asked the bartender if he wasn't bothered by such odd behavior. The bartender, who had described the story in a flat voice, as if he was talking about the weather, responded, "Hell, no-she's a lot less trouble than a lot of the broads you get in here." The suspect was ultimately convicted of the death of a prostitute although he was suspected in a number of other murders.

(**Note:** the identity of the suspect, including the state of residence, remains undisclosed as I had the occasion to interview the individual over the course of time. The offender had a history of firesetting behavior, starting at age four, as best he could recall, associated with a belief that setting a fire helped him "stay calm". He acknowledged that his firesetting had always been a secret and that as he got older, he "always" set a fire after masturbation and that, "It was just part of it, that's all." He admitted to sadistic fantasies that gave him a great deal of pleasure and that he "Always kept a secret place wherever I live at the time." specific to masturbation. He admitted to setting "A little fire after, just in an ashtray, no big deal. It just ends it, that's all." He denied any involvement in sexual assaults or homicide. He is currently serving a lengthy sentence.)

Interrogation Strategies for Police and Fire Investigators

Disordered coping firesetters have kept secrets for many years and have no desire to unburden themselves. Lacking guilt, they usually also lack anxiety, and their success at any past criminal activity gives them a general feeling of confidence. It is important to recognize that this firesetter subtype has many of the features of the psychopath described at length in Chapter 6. However, generally speaking, they are not narcissistic in their demeanor and do not regard interrogation as a game.

It is important to gather as much background on the life of this subtype as possible before you undertake an interrogation. Your strength will come from making the suspect believe that you know all about him, including his locked room. This is unnerving to an individual who has lived a secret life and may serve to unbalance him. We believe it is a waste of time to use a typical "good cop, bad cop" strategy as the suspect will not bond to the good cop and will remain silent with the bad cop.

This kind of suspect demands that you keep two things in mind-you are most probably facing someone who may be a sex offender as well as an arsonist. In fact, we venture to say that if you are conducting an interrogation, it is more likely because of a sex offense rather than a case of arson. Because the disordered coping subtype set fires to feel better and restore a sense of emotional equilibrium, their activity may account for hundreds of fires of all sizes and at various locations starting in childhood and occurring throughout adult life. They do not generally have specific targets, as do revenge setters, or visit the scene before the event, as do thrill seekers. Their firesetting is unpredictable in its scope and degree of dangerousness and relates to a need to feel better at a particular moment in time. It is important from an investigative standpoint to recognize that disordered coping arsonists do not remain behind to watch their fires, do not follow their fires in the media, do not brag about their fires to friends, as they generally have no friend, and feel no need to unburden their souls. What is characteristic, however, is that after a fire is set, this type of arsonist simply walks away without thought of discovery.

In adulthood, it is not unusual for disordered coping arsonists to be married. Their choice of partners is interesting as they seem to select women who dislike physical contact and have little use for sexual interaction. This dynamic is often of great comfort to the subtype as they report impotency without the presence of sadistic fantasies and behaviors. Most of the men we have interviewed over the past twenty years have disclosed that they do not involve their wives in sadism and a number have been offended that we even mentioned the possibility.

We suggest that, if possible, the interrogation team should be comprised of male officers only. The presence of female officers may engender preoccupation with sadistic fantasies that cannot be used to your advantage as the suspect has no reason to disclose the content to you. Remember that the suspect has many of the qualities you would associate with a psychopath, so attempting to elicit his empathy for victims, including the impact of the crimes on his own family, is futile. He does not understand the suffering of another and cannot care about it. His victims have no meaning to him. He does not feel that society should be protected from him as he pays no attention to the needs of society.

We recommend that you begin with a presumption of wrong-doing. In other words, you do not ask if the suspect committed the crime, you state your knowledge of guilt as a given. If you obtain a confession at all, lacking direct physical evidence, it might be elicited through your spoken desire to understand the reason for the crime—and remember, with the disordered coping subtype, the crime might be sexual assault and arson. Maintain a neutral posture and attitude and do not express surprise at any possible disclosure. Whatever you learn may be the proverbial tip of the iceberg.

Chapter 8

Conclusions and Thoughts

Writing this book has been a challenging endeavor for me. So much of what is presented herein is not based in the language of hard science but instead reflects knowledge and experience with a particular set of behaviors. To that end, it is a narrow book and its intent is not to answer every possible question about the behavior and motivation of arsonists. As with all true research, it is a work in progress. The intent of the text is best understood as a "how-to" resource for those investigators and students of deviance who work in the field. Over the years, I have been impressed at the dedication of criminal justice and fire investigators desperate to get dangerous arsonists off the streets, through incarceration or treatment, or if possible, through early recognition and intervention. All too often, we at The Center for Arson Research encounter the results of failed or missed attempts at intervention. As we have learned over the years, much of what is been written about firesetters does not seem to apply to the forensic population—the conclusions often seem much too broad or paradoxically, much too narrow to be of real use. Additionally, although some of the scientific literature on firesetting may be sound, it is often too technical and difficult to follow for readers not grounded in social statistics.

There are firesetting subtypes we recognize that this text has not addressed, based in part on my decision not to review a larger population than offered in the original random sample of 310 subjects. To that end, I elected not to discuss cluster setters (fires set around an anniversary date of some personal traumatic loss), fraud arsonists (fires set for profit) or female firesetters at any length in all subtypes. My plan is to discuss those subtypes in a larger total sample of 500 firesetters in the second edition of the text.

145

As I thought about it, I decided that a chapter on female firesetters deserved a larger sample than the 32 female clients in the cohort found in this book. My plan is to expand the sample and offer more comprehensive data on female firesetters related to a broader look at the concept of female criminality. The study of women and crime has attracted increased research attention over the past several decades. Gender-based findings that females commit fewer crimes than males, overall, have historically been squarely placed at the feet of socialization differences. Such findings presume that females are socialized to behave less aggressively than males.

Females are more likely to turn aggressive feelings and impulses inward while males externalize them and respond aggressively to others (Mirowsky & Ross, 1995). Some theorists posit that females who commit crimes of violence are more likely than males to have troubled family relationships (Hoge, Andrews, & Leschied, 1994). However, there are other theorists who believe that factors affecting and predisposing male crime should have the same effect on female crime rates. Feminist theories of crime support the notion that the imbalance of power between males and females in our society account for the gender-based differences in crime rates (Messerschmidt, 1986). Still, various explanations of the rates and causes of female crime do not adequately explain why females (if powerless) do not have higher rates of crime, as is the case with other perceived powerless groups, such as found in the over-represented socio-economically deprived members of society.

Our study of firesetting behavior in females finds that, overall, the reasons that lead males to set fires are the same reasons that females set fires. From a basic research perspective, however, the fascinating variable that we cannot explain to our satisfaction is why female firesetting generally disappears (in all subtypes) while male firesetting may continue over the course of a lifetime. At its most basic and simple, the explanation could well be the widely held notion that females are socialized out of aggressive behavior.

More importantly, from our perspective, is that even in the disordered coping subtype, where the use of fire is a primary learned response to stress, girls seem to make an adjustment to other behaviors as they mature. The shift from firesetting to other behaviors (often self-destructive) occurs around the onset of puberty in most girls but not nearly as often in boys. The need to look at observable implications of this finding calls for more testing of the theory around the motivation for firesetting with additional and more varied data collection.

One notable exception to firesetting behavior is found in the revenge subtype where we see female firesetters almost always as adults. Our small and admittedly inadequate sample for this text, offered only as a point of discussion, indicates that the females had an average age of eighteen at the time of their evaluations, considerably older than males in all subtypes.

Female revenge arsonists set fires after some experience of an unexpected loss or rejection. Because the loss occurs without warning, women who set fires appear to experience a sudden disruption of emotional equilibrium, accompanied by a feeling of intense rage. An example of a female revenge fire might be found in the following account: A wife learns after thirty years of marriage that her husband is leaving her for a (much) younger woman. This news is unexpected and overwhelmingly devastating; she reacts by gathering all his belongings, throwing them on the bed, and setting them ablaze. Before she knows it, the home is engulfed in flame and within twenty minutes, her house is destroyed.

Her act of revenge, directed at her husband's things, was not planned as a destructive arson fire. It was conceived in haste and rage and directed at hurting him through the things he valued. It is clear to us when interviewing such a client, that (if I may make this distinction) her intent was not criminal but retaliatory and personal. A hallmark of such an arson fire is that the setter has no criminal history, and as we have found on most occasions, until that event, no anger management problems, either. Firesetting behavior, occurring in an adult female under extreme provocation and with no mental health or criminal justice history, has an extremely small chance of ever reoccurring.

We find females under-represented in all other fire subtypes as well. Males do set a disproportionate share of fires and even when females are firesetters, they tend to relinquish that behavior much sooner than males, even when no intervention is present. In a number of subtypes, such as thrill seekers, females are virtually nonexistent, as far as we know. The topic of females and firesetting continues to be understudied overall.

There are many gaps in knowledge about the development of, and intervention strategies for, firesetting behavior across the subtypes. Motivation is still not clearly understood and researchers continue frequently enough to mix emotions (excitement), diagnosis (conduct disorder) and intellectual levels (mental retardation) together, for example, as possible explanations for why individuals start fires. New research, re-examination of existing studies or additional data added to existing studies would serve to enhance knowledge about firesetting.

Many early studies were based around data collected on adult male offenders and extrapolated to all other firesetters, leading to faulty conclusions. A fair criticism of research on firesetters is that it frequently compares firesetters with non-firesetters, such as individuals without firesetting histories receiving outpatient services at the same clinic location. Perhaps more comprehensive studies could compare firesetters with firesetters to study motivation, the risk for continued firesetting associated with motivation, and intervention strategies that appear successful in each subtype through comprehensive longitudinal research. Although firesetting may be one of only many delinquent or criminal behaviors present in an individual, there are also others who have no history of any aberrant or dangerous behavior besides setting fires.

A social science theory is a reasoned explanation that responds to a proposed question and is based, in part, on work already done elsewhere on the subject. King, Keohane and Verba (1994) advise social science researchers to select a theory that could be wrong and direct attention to learning what you can from it. An example of that premise for those of us at the Center for Arson Research could be found in the data we collected for at least fourteen years on the variable of nocturnal enuresis (bedwetting).

Seminal work by Freud (1932) who treated four male clients with histories of setting fires and other orthodox analysts such as Fenichel (1945) proposed that a perverse relationship existed between enuresis and firesetting, essentially through their analysis of dream states. Early writing on firesetters associated the behaviors of sexual deviance and urination for pleasure (Gold, 1962; Lewis & Yarnell, 1951). Such conclusions established an association between fire, erotic pleasure, and bedwetting and the three elements became part of the mythology of the arsonist.

I began my work with firesetting behavior by a careful review of the scholarly literature available on firesetting in the late 1970s. Early findings seemed to support later research and although I was somewhat puzzled at the mix of motivations, I accepted the research, overall. It was not until much later that I understood how much of the data related to studies of adult offenders, extrapolated to youth, and revolved around record reviews or small samples, many without controls. One of the variables mentioned in virtually every study on firesetters was of the finding of nocturnal enuresis. With that in mind, as I developed our first questionnaire and the next two versions, we collected data on bedwetting for fourteen years.

The Center for Arson Research questionnaire allows the collection of data through open-ended and swing questions, allowing each interviewee a full opportunity to explain his or her responses. No judgment or interpretation is made of any response at the time of the interview. We consider it important to gather the individual's subjective understanding of the questions. Clarification is provided for any question, if requested or if it appears the client does not understand what is being asked. Information is written down by the interviewer as the client speaks and the client is invited to read, or have read, what the interviewer records. Responses are then cross-referenced with other supportive documentation, if available, and through discussions with treatment providers, criminal or juvenile justice staff and other vested parties.

The results of data collection around the variable of bedwetting resulted in a positive response in approximately 7 percent of the total population of firesetters in all subtypes and I made the decision to stop collecting that information. There were two reasons for the decision, one was the meager result but the second reason (and the more important one) was that the presence or absence of bedwetting seemed to have no relationship to the level of dangerousness of the firesetter, the subtype, or the motivation for setting fires. We recognize that some social scientists view data on bedwetting as of importance and believe that each researcher determines particular areas of concentration and study.

The Research Agenda

There are many gaps in knowledge about the development and continuation of firesetting behavior at different life stages. While some theorists report tremendous results with specific therapeutic interventions, we often see the individuals at a later point in their lives for whom strategic interventions failed. Evaluators at the Center also respond to requests for follow up interviews in clients who are declared "fire free" only to determine that firesetting has continued, undetected or undisclosed all along. We believe more research is needed on what are the most useful typologies of firesetter motivations in order to lead us to more successful strategies for intervention, prevention, assessment and treatment.

More research is certainly needed on treatment intervention strategies particularly for firesetters who fit into the subtypes related to setting fires for excitement, for revenge and as a means of coping. We are fairly confident that the interventions now used by practitioners for the interruption of delinquent conduct are equally applicable for delinquents who set fires, as fire appears to be just another negative behavior of delinquency. An issue of importance is how the more serious and dangerous firesetters differ from youth who seem to grow up and out of firesetting as they grow up and out of delinquency, despite many of the youth sharing the same kinds of history to a greater or lesser degree.

More social science research is necessary to identify and clarify any developmental pathways that seem to influence the progression of deviant offending in firesetters. Popularly, it is acceptable to attribute serious and violent behavior to a history of victimization previously suffered by the offender. Although there are a disproportionate number of self-reports of victimization in firesetters, across the subtypes, there are also firesetters without a history of maltreatment. It seems important to study the effects of other possible social variables that may impact on firesetting behavior, such as poverty, placement outside the home and family mental health. Additionally there is a need to study possible biochemical and neurological findings in those who set ongoing fires without regard to possible consequences for self or others.

Our Future Plans

The Center for Arson Research staff will begin to assess additional data starting in January, 2005. We are interested in exploring in greater depth how many, and to what degree, the clients we interview have had exposure to domestic violence, either as victims or witnesses. We plan to review formats used to assess sex offenders for continued risk and modify them as needed to further clarify risk characteristics in firesetters. After gathering data from the risk assessment tool, we will design a risk factor instrument that can be used to determine levels of care and appropriate intervention strategies.

We believe that early recognition and appropriate intervention are the keys to interrupting firesetting behavior. We are hopeful that more programs will devote specific treatment opportunities to develop an understanding of firesetting behavior. Longitudinal studies are essential by treatment providers and the justice system in collecting follow-up data on clients who have participated in intervention, rehabilitation, incarceration and/or education programs. Our vision of the future is rooted in the past. Every day we learn more than we knew before about firesetting behavior. We believe that research and intervention are integral in the interruption of firesetting behavior.

References

Aber, J. & Allen, J.P. (1987). Effect of maltreatment on young children's socioemotional development: An attachment theory perspective. *Developmental Psychology*, 23(3), 406-414.

Abel, G., Becker, J., Blanchard, E. & Djenderedjian, A. (1978). Differentiating sexual aggressives with penile measures. *Criminal Justice and Behavior*, 5, 315-332.

Abel, G., Becker, J., Blanchard, E.,, & Guild, D. (1977). The components of rapists' sexual arousal. *Archives of General Psychiatry*, 34, 895-903.

Adler, F., Mueller, G., & Laufer, W. (1998). *Criminology, the shorter version.* (3rd ed.). Boston: McGraw Hill.

Adler, R., Nunn, R., Northam, E., Lebnan, V., & Ross, R. (1994). Secondary prevention of childhood firesetting. *Journal of the American Academy of Child and Adolescent Psychiatry*, 33, 1194-1202.

Akers, R. (1997). *Criminological theories, introduction and evaluation* (2nd ed.). Los Angeles, CA: Roxbury.

American Psychiatric Association. (1994). *Diagnostic and statistical manual of mental disorders* (IV). (4th ed.). Washington, DC: Author.

Ammerman, R., Cassisi, J.E., Hersen, M. & Van Hasselt, V. B. (1986). Consequences of physical abuse and neglect in children. *Clinical Psychology Review*, 6, 291-310.

Andreasen, N. C. & Carpenter, W. (1993). Diagnosis and classification of schizophrenia. *Schizophrenia Bulletin*, 19, 199-214.

Anscombe, R. (1987). The disorder of consciousness in schizophrenia. *Schizophrenia Bulletin*, 13(2), 241-259.

Anthony, E.J. & Koupernik, C. (Eds.). (1974). *The child in his family: Children at psychiatric risk*, Vol. 3. New York: Wiley.

Antisocial personality—Part 1. (2000, Dec.). *Harvard Mental Health Letter*, 17, 6.

Arieti, S. (1980, October). Psychotherapy of schizophrenia: New or revised procedures. *American Journal of Psychotherapy*, 34, 464-476.

Arrigo, B. (2000). Critical criminology and social justice: On integrating knowledge. *Contemporary Justice Review*, 3(1), 7-37.

Ball, A., Farnill, D., & Wangeman, J. (1984). Sex and age differences in sensation seeking: Some national comparisons. *British Journal of Psychology*, 75, 257-265.

Bandura, A. (1977). Self-efficiency: Towards a unifying theory of behavioral change. *Psychological Review*, 84, 191-215.

Bandura, A. (1973). *Aggression: A social learning analysis.* Englewood Cliffs, NJ: Prentice Hall.

Bandura, A. & Waller, (1959). *Adolescent aggression.* New York: Ronald Press.

Barkan, S. & Snowden, L. (2001). *Collective violence.* Needham Heights, MA: Allyn and Bacon.

Barker, A. (1994). Arson: A review of the psychiatric literature. *Maudsley Monographs*, 35, 1-98.

Bartol, C. (2002). *Criminal behavior: A psychosocial approach.* (6th ed.). Upper Saddle River, NJ: Prentice Hall.

Bartol, C. & Bartol, A. (2005). *Criminal behavior: A psychosocial approach.* (7th ed.). Upper Saddle River, NJ: Pearson/Prentice Hall.

Bench, L., Kramer, S.P., Erikson, S. (1997). A discriminant analysis of predictive factors in sex offender recidivism. In B.K. Schwartz & H.R. Cellini (Eds.), *The sex offender: New insights, treatment innovations and legal developments*, 15.1-15.15. Kingston, NJ: Civic Research Institute.

Bergman, S. J., Larsen, R., & Mueller, B. (1986). Changing spectrum of serious child abuse. *Pediatrics*, 77(1), 113-116.

Berry, R. (1993, November). Effective patient education, part 2: Teaching children. *Nursing Spectrum*, 14-15.

Bilchik, S. (1999, July). *Report to Congress on juvenile violence research*. Washington, DC: U.S. Department of Justice.

Blackburn, R. (1993). *The psychology of criminal conduct: Theory, research and practice*. Chichester, Eng.: Wiley.

Block, J. & Block, J. (1980). The role of ego-control and ego resiliency in the organization of behavior. In W.A. Collins (Ed.), *Minnesota Symposia on Child Psychology: Vol. 13*. Development of cognition, affect, and social relations, 39-101. Hillsdale, NJ: Erlbaum.

Block, J., Block, J.H. & Keyes, S. (1988). Longitudinally foretelling drug usage in adolescence: Early childhood personality and environmental precursors. *Child Development*, 59, 336-355.

Blumberg, N. (1981). Arson update: A review of the literature on firesetting. *Bulletin of the American Academy of Psychiatry & the Law*, 9(4), 255-265.

Blumstein, A. (2001, February). Why is crime falling-or is it? In *Perspectives on Crime and Justice: 2000-2001 Lecture Series* (Vol 5, March, 2002). Washington, DC: National Institute of Justice.

Bohm, R. & Haley, K. (1997). *Introduction to criminal justice*. New York: McGraw Hill.

Boisvert, M. (1972, October). The battered child syndrome. *Social Casework*, 53, 475-481.

Bourget, D. & Bradford, J.M. (1989). Female arsonists: A clinical study. *Bulletin of the American Academy of Psychiatry & the Law*, 17(3), 293-300.

Brady, J. (1983). Arson, urban economy, and organized crime: The case of Boston. *Social Problems*, 31, 1-27.

Braig, A. & Whelan, R. (1995). *Juvenile Firesetter Education and Prevention Program*. Camden County Fire Marshal's Office. Blackwood: NJ.

Bronson, M. (2000). *Self-regulation in early childhood: Nature and nurture*. New York: Guilford Press.

Brppke, J. (1996, July 5). Volatile mix in Viper Militia: Hatred plus a love for guns. *New York Times*, p. 1.

Brooker, C. (1990). A new role for the community psychiatric nurse in working with families caring for a relative with schizophrenia. *The International Journal of Social Psychiatry*, 36 (3), 216-224.

Brown, S., Glegham, A., Schuckit, M.A., Myers, M. & Mott, M. (1996). Conduct disorder among adolescent alcohol and drug users. *Journal of Studies on Alcohol*, 57, 314-324.

Bureau of Justice Statistics (2002). *Crime victimization in the United States, 2001 statistical tables: National crime victimization survey.* Washington, DC: Department of Justice, Bureau of Justice Statistics.

Cameron, N. (1963). *Personality development and psychopathology.* Boston: Houghton Mifflin.

Cancro, R. (1978). *The healer and madness.* (Strecker Monograph Series, No. 15). The Fifteenth Institute of Pennsylvania Hospital Award Lecture.

Cancro, R. (1983, October). Individual psychotherapy in the treatment of chronic schizophrenic patients. *American Journal of Psychotherapy*, 37, 493-501.

Carroll, J. & Rest, J.R. (1982). Moral development. In B. Wolman (ed.). *Handbook of Developmental Psychology* Englewood Cliffs, NJ: Prentice- Hall.

Chaiken, M.R. (1998). *Violent neighborhoods-violent kids: What could be done with boys in D.C.* Alexandria, VA: Linc.

Cleckley, H. (1982). *The mask of sanity* (5th ed.). St. Louis, MO: Mosby.

Conger, J. & Miller, W. (1966). *Personality, social class, and delinquency.* New York: Wiley.

Conn, V. (1990). Commentary: The case against family systems theory. *Journal of Child and Adolescent Psychiatric and Mental Health Nursing*, 3 (1), 29-33.

Cowley, G. (1993, July). The not-young and the restless. *Newsweek*, 48-49.

Cox-Jones, C., Lubetsky, M., Fultz, S.A. & Kolko, D. (1990). Case study: Inpatient psychiatric treatment of a young recidivist firesetter. *Journal of the American Academy of Child and Adolescent Psychiatry*, 29(6), 936-941.

Cressey, D. (1970). Organized crime and inner city youth. *Crime and Delinquency*,16, 129-138.

Curra, J. (2000). *The relativity of deviance.* Thousand Oaks, CA: Sage.

Davidson, J. & Smith, R. (1990). Traumatic experiences in psychiatric outpatients. *Journal of Traumatic Stress*, 3(3), 459-475.

Davis, R. (2003, November). Mental health of US prisoners is poor. *Lancet*, 362, 9349, p. 1466.

Denno, D. (1985). Sociological and human developmental explanations of crime: Conflict or consensus. *Criminology*, 23, 711-741.

Deykin, E., Levy, J.C.,& Wells, V. (1987). Adolescent depression: Alcohol and drug use. *American Journal of Public Health*, 77(2), 178-182.

DiLalla, L.F. & Gottesman, I. (1991). Biological and genetic contributions to violence: Widom's untold tale. *Psychological Bulletin*, 109, 125-129.

Dodge, K., Bates, J.E., & Pettit, G. (1990). Mechanisms in the cycle of violence. *Science*, 250, 1678-1683.

Durkheim, E. (1997). *The division of labor in society* (reprint ed.). New York: Free Press.

Egan, K. (1983). Stress management and child management with abusive parents. *Journal of Clinical Child Psychology*, 12, 292-299.

Egeland, B. (1993). A history of abuse is a major risk factor for abusing the next generation. In R. Gelles & D. Loseke (Eds.), *Current controversies on family violence* (pp. 197-208). Newbury Park, CA: Sage.

Einbender, A. J., & Friedrich, W. (1989). Psychological functioning and behavior of sexually abused girls. *Journal of Consulting and Clinical Psychology*. 57(1), 155-157.

Elliott, D. (1994). Serious violent offenders: Onset, developmental course, and termination-the American Society of Criminology 1993 presidential address. *Criminology*, 32, 1-21.

Elliot, M. (1992). *Bullying: A practical guide to coping for schools*. Harlow, Longman.

Elmer, E. (1977). Follow-up study of traumatized children. *Pediatrics*, 59, 272-279.

Emery, R.E. (1989). Family violence. *American Psychologist*, 44(2), 321-328.

Emotional expression in criminals. (2002, Feb.). *Harvard Mental Health Letter*, 18 (8), p. 8.

Epstein, M. & Bottoms, B. (1998). Memories of childhood sexual abuse: A survey of young adults. *Child Abuse & Neglect*, 22(12), 1217-1238.

Erez, E. & Tontodonato, P. (1989). Patterns of reported parent-child abuse and police response. *Journal of Family Violence*, 4, 143-159.

Erikson, E. H. (1950). *Childhood and society*. New York: W. W. Norton.

Erikson, E. H. (1968). *Identity, youth and crisis*. New York: W.W. Norton.

Eysenck, H. (1977). *Crime and personality*. London: Routledge Kegan Paul.

Farrington, D. (1989). Early predictors of adolescent aggression and adult violence. *Violence and Victims*, 4, 79-100.

Farrington, D. (1991). Childhood aggression and adult violence: Early precursors and later life outcomes. In D. Pepler & K.H.Rubin (Eds.). *The development and treatment of childhood aggression*. Hillsdale, NJ: Erlbaum.

Federal Bureau of Investigation. (1994). Crime in the United States. *FBI Uniform Crime Reports*. Washington, DC:U. S. Government Printing Office.

Federal Bureau of Investigation. (1997). Crime in the United States. *FBI Uniform Crime Reports*. Washington, DC: U.S. Government Printing Office.

Federal Bureau of Investigation. (2000). Crime in the United States. *FBI Uniform Crime Reports*. Washington, DC: U.S. Government Printing Office.

Federal Bureau of Investigation. (2001). Crime in the United States. *FBI Uniform Crime Reports*. Washington, DC: U.S. Government Printing Office.

Federal Emergency Management Agency (2003). *Firefighter arson: Special report*. Emmitsburg, MD: US Fire Administration.

Feldman, S. & Weinberger, D.A. (1994). Self-restraint as a mediator of family influences on boys' delinquent behavior: A longitudinal study. *Child Development*, 65, 195-211.

Felson, M. & Cohen, L. (1980). Human ecology and crime: A routine activity approach. *Human Ecology*, 8(4), 389-406.

Fenichel, O. (1945). *The psychoanalytic theory of neurosis*. New York: W.W. Norton.

Fineman, K. (1980). Firesetting in childhood and adolescence. *Psychiatric Clinics of North America*, 3, 483-500.

Frazier, S. & Carr, A. (1964). *Introduction to psychopathology.* New York: MacMillan.

Freud, S. (1946). *The ego and the mechanisms of defense.* NY: International Universities Press.

Freud, S. (1970). *Three case histories.* New York: Macmillan Collier.

Gaines, L., Kaune, M. & Miller, R. (2001). *Criminal justice in action.* Belmont, CA: Wadsworth/Thomson Learning.

Garmezy, N. ((1983). Stressors of childhood. In N. Garmezy (Ed.), *Stress, coping, and development in children*, 43-84. New York: McGraw-Hill.

Gaynor, J. & Hatcher, C. (1987). *The psychology of child firesetting: Detection and intervention.* New York: Brunner/Mazel.

Geller, J. (1992). Arson in review: From profit to pathology. *Clinical Forensic Psychiatry*, 15(3), 623-645.

Gelles, R. (1987). The family and its role in abuse of children. *Psychiatric Annals*, 17, 229-232.

Gelles, R. & Conte, J. (1990, November). Domestic violence and sexual abuse of children: A review of research in the eighties. *Journal of Marriage and the Family*, 52, 1045-1058.

Gelles, R. & Strauss, U. (1987, June). Is violence towards children increasing? *Journal of Interpersonal Violence*, 2, 212-223.

Gesell, A. & Ilg, F. (1946). *The child from five to ten.* New York: Harper & Row.

Gil, D. (1979). *Violence against children.* Cambridge, MA: Harvard University Press.

Gilbert, J. (1986). *Criminal investigation.* (2nd ed.). Columbus, Ohio: Charles Merrill.

Gilligan, C. (1982). *In a different voice: Psychological theory and women's development.* Cambridge, MA.: Harvard University Press.

Gilmore, S. (2004, August 4). Arson experts say firebug is thrill seeker. *The Seattle Times*, 1.

Giordano, P., Cernkovich, S. & Pugh, M.D. (1986). Friendships and delinquency. *American Journal of Sociology* 91, 1170-1202.

Giovannano, J. & Billingsley, A. (1970). Child neglect among the poor. *Child Welfare*, 49, 196-204.

Glueck, S. & Glueck, E. (1959). *Predicting delinquency and crime*. Cambridge, MA: Harvard University Press.

Gold, L.H. (1962). Psychiatric profile of the firesetter. *Journal of Forensic Sciences*, 7, 404-417.

Gold, M. (1978). School experiences, self-esteem, and delinquent behavior: A theory in alternative schools. *Crime and Delinquency*, 24, 294-295.

Gottesman, II, McGuffin, P., & Farmer, A. (1987). Clinical genetics as clues to the "real" genetics of schizophrenia (A decade of modest gains while playing for time). *Schizophrenia Bulletin*, 13(1), 23-47.

Groth, N. & Birnbaum, J. (1979). *Men who rape: The psychology of the offender*. New York: Plenum Press.

Gruber, A., Heck, E.T. & Mintzer, E. (1981). Children who set fires: Some background and behavioral characteristics. *American Journal of Orthopsychiatry*, 51, 484-488.

Guerra, N., Huesmann, L., Tolan, P.H., & Eron, L. (1995). Stressful events and individual beliefs as correlates of economic disadvantage and aggression among urban children. *Journal of Consulting and Clinical Psychology*, 63, 518-528.

Hafner, H. & Boker, W. (1982). *Crimes of violence by mentally disordered offenders*. Cambridge, England: Cambridge University Press.

Halleck, S. (1967). *Psychiatry and the dilemmas of crime*. New York: Harper & Row, p. 194.

Hamparian, D., Davis, J., Jacobson, J. & McGraw, R. (1985). *The young criminal years of the violent few*. National institute of Juvenile Justice and Delinquency Prevention. Washington, DC: U.S. Department of Justice.

Hampton, R. (1987). Race, class and child maltreatment. *Journal of Comparative Family Studies*, 18, 113-126.

Hampton, R. & Newberger, E.H. (1985). Hospitals as gatekeepers: Recognition and reporting in the national incidence study of child abuse and neglect. *Report to National Center on Child Abuse and Neglect*. Children's Bureau, Administration for Children, Youth and Families. Washington, DC: US Department of Health and Human Services.

Hanson, R.K., & Harris, A. (2000). Where should we intervene? Dynamic predictors of sexual offense recidivism. *Criminal Justice and Behavior*, 27, 6-35.

Hanson. M., MacKay-Soroka, S. & Staley, S. (1994). Delinquent firesetters: A comparative study of delinquent and firesetting histories. *Canadian Journal of Psychiatry*, 39(4), 230-232.

Harris, G. & Rice, M. (1996, September). A typology of mentally disordered firesetters. *Journal of Interpersonal Violence*, 11 (3), 351-363.

Hare, R. (1970). *Psychopathy: Theory and research*. New York: Wiley.

Hare, R. (1993). *Without conscience: The disturbing world of the psychopaths among us*. New York: Guilford Press.

Haskett, M. E. & Kistner, J. (1991). Social interactions and peer perceptions of young physically abused children. *Child Development*, 62, 979-990.

Heath, G., Hardesty, V., Goldfine, P. & Walker, A. (1985). Diagnosis and childhood firesetting. *Journal of Clinical Psychology*, 41(4), 571-575.

Helfer, R. & Kempe, C.H. (1972). *Helping the battered child and his family*. Philadelphia: J.B. Lippincott.

Heide, K. M. (1995). *Why kids kill parents: Child abuse and adolescent homicide*. Thousand Oaks, CA: Sage.

Heindl, C., Krall, C., Salus, M., & Broadhurst, D. (1979). *The nurse's role in the prevention and treatment of child abuse and neglect*. Washington, DC: HEW Publication.

Henker, B. & Whalen, C. (1989). Hyperactivity and attention deficits. *American Psychologist*, 44, 216-244.

Henn, F., Herjanic, M. & Vanderpearl, R.H. (1976). Forensic psychiatry: Profiles of two types of sex offenders. *American Journal of Psychiatry*, 133, 694-696.

Hirschi, T. (1969). *Causes of delinquency*. Berkeley: University of California Press.

Hirschi, T. & Hindelang, M. (1977). Intelligence and delinquency: A revisionist review. *American Sociological Review*, 42, 571-586.

Hochstedler Steury, E. (1993). Criminal defendants with psychiatric impairment: Prevalence, probabilities and rates. *Journal of Criminal Law and Criminology*, 84, 354-374.

Hoge, R., Andrews, D., & Leschied, A. (1994). Tests of three hypotheses regarding the predictors of delinquency. *Journal of Abnormal Child Psychology*, 22, 547-559.

Huba, G., Wingard, J. & Bentler, P. (1979). Beginning adolescent drug use and peer and adult interaction patterns. *Journal of Consulting Clinical Psychology*, 47, 265-276.

Huff, T., Gary, G., & Icove, D. (1997). *The myth of pyromania*. National Center for the Analysis of Violent Crime. Washington, DC: Federal Bureau of Investigation, Department of Justice.

Huizinga, D. & Elliott, D. (1987). Juvenile offenders: Prevalence, offender incidence, and arrest rates by race. *Crime and Delinquency*, 33, 206-223.

Inciardi, J. (1996). *Criminal justice* (5th ed.). Ft. Worth: Harcourt Brace.

Inciardi, J. (1997). *Elements of criminal justice*. Fort Worth: Harcourt Brace.

Ireland, T. & Spatz Widom, C. (1995). *Childhood victimization and risk for alcohol and drug arrests*. Washington, DC: National Institute for Justice.

Jackson, P. G. (1988). Assessing the validity of official data on arson. *Criminology*, 26(1), 181-195.

Jacobson, E. (1971). *Depression*. New York: International Universities Press.

Jacobson, R.R. (1985). The subclassification of child firesetters. *American Journal of Orthopsychiatry*, 16, 84-94.

Jensen, G. & Rojek, D. (1992). *Delinquency and youth crime*. (2nd ed.). Prospect Heights, IL: Waveland Press.

Jessor, R. & Jessor, S. (1977). *Problem behavior and psychosocial development: A longitudinal study of youth.* New York: Academic Press.

Johnson, B. (1993). *Adaptation and growth: Psychiatric mental health nursing.* (3rd. ed.). Philadelphia: J.B. Lippincott.

Johnson, R., Su, S., Gerstein, D., Shin, H-C, & Hoffman, J. (1995). Parental influences on deviant behavior in early adolescence: A logistic response analysis of age and gender differentiated effects. *Journal of Quantitative Criminology*, 11, 167-192.

Jongsma, A., Peterson, L.M., & McInnis, W. (1996). *The child and adolescent psychotherapy treatment planner.* New York: John Wiley & Sons.

Jurgensmeyer, M. (2000). *Terror in the mind of God.* Los Angeles: University of CA Press.

Justice, B. & Justice, R. (1976). *The abusing family.* New York: Human Sciences Press.

Kallman, F. (1953). *Heredity in health and mental disorders.* New York: W.W. Norton,

Kandel, D., Kessler, R., & Marguilies, R. (1978). Antecedents of adolescent initiation into stages of drug use: A developmental analysis. *Journal of Youth and Adolescence*, 7, 13-40.

Kaplan, H. (1980). *Deviant behavior in defense of self.* New York: Academic Press.

Karter, M. (1994). Fire loss in the United States in 1993. *NFPA Journal*,88, 59-64.

Kasen, S., Cohen, P., Skodol, AE, Johnson, JG, & Brook, J. (1999). Influences of child and adolescent psychiatric disorders on young adult personality disorder. *American Journal of Psychiatry*, 156, 1529-1535.

Kazdin, A. E. (1985). *Treatment of antisocial behavior in children and adolescence.* Homewood, IL: Dorsey Press.

Kelley, B., Thornberry, T. P., & Smith, C. (1997, August). In the wake of childhood maltreatment. *Juvenile Justice Bulletin.* Washington, DC: US Department of Justice.

Kelso, J. & Stewart, M. (1986). Factors which predict the persistence of aggressive conduct disorder. *Journal of Child Psychology and Psychiatry and Allied Disciplines*, 27(1), 77-86.

Kendall-Tackett, K.A., Williams, L.M. & Finklehor, D. (1993). Impact of sexual abuse on children: A review and synthesis of recent empirical studies. *Psychological Bulletin*, 113(1), 164-180.

Kessler, R., McGonagle, K.A., Ahzo, S., Nelson, C.H., Hughes, M., Eshleman, S., Wittchen, H., & Kendler, K. (1994). Lifetime and 12-month prevalence of DSM-III-R psychiatric disorders in the United States. *Archives of General Psychiatry*, 51, 8-19.

King, G., Keohane, R. & Verba, S. (1994). *Designing social inquiry: Scientific inference in qualitative research*. Princeton, NJ: Princeton University Press.

Klinteberg, B., Magnusson, D. & Schalling, D. (1989). Hyperactive behavior in childhood and adult impulsivity: A longitudinal study of male subjects. *Personality and Individual Differences*, 10, 43-50.

Knight, R. (1937). The psychodynamics of chronic alcoholism. *Journal of Nervous and Mental Diseases*. 86, 538-548.

Knight, R.A., Prentky, R.A., & Cerce, D.D. (1994). The development, reliability, and validity of an inventory for the multidimensional assessment of sex and aggression. *Criminal Justice and Behavior*, 21, 72-94.

Kohlberg, L. (1969). *Stages in the development of moral thought and action*. New York: Holt, Rinehart and Winston.

Kohlberg, L. (1973). Continuities in childhood and adult moral development revisited. In P. Baltes & K.W. Schaie (Eds.), *Life-span developmental psychology: Personality and socialization*. New York: Academic Press.

Kolko, D. (1985). Juvenile firesetting: A review and methodological critique. *Clinical Psychology Review*, 5, 345-375.

Kolko, D. & Kadzin, A. (1991). Aggression and psychopathology in matchplaying and firesetting children: A replication and extension. *Journal of Clinical Child Psychology and Psychiatry*, 18, 191-201.

Kopp, C. B. (1982). Antecedents of self-regulation: A developmental perspective. *Developmental Psychology*, 18, 199-214.

Kosky, R. & Silburn, S. (1984). Children who light fires: A comparison between firesetters and nonfiresetters referred to a child psychiatric outpatient service. *Journal of Child Psychology and Psychiatry*, 18, 251-255.

Kraepelin, E. (1976). *Manic depressive insanity and paranoia*. New York: Arno Press.

Krug, E., Dahlberg, L., Mercy, J., Zwi, A. & Lozano, R. (2002). *World Report on Violence and Health*. Geneva: World Health Organization.

Kruttschnitt, C., McLeod, J. & Dornfeld, M. (1994). The economic environment of child abuse. *Social Problems*, 41, 299-315.

Kuhnley, E.J. & Hendren, R., & Quinlan, D. (1982). Firesetting by children. *Journal of the American Academy of Child Psychiatry*, 21, 560-563.

Laws, D. & Marshall, W.L. (1990). A conditioning theory of the etiology and maintenance of deviant sexual preference and behavior. In W.L. Marshall, D. Laws, and H.E. Barabaree (Eds.), *Handbook of sexual assault*. New York: Plenum Press.

Lazarus, R. S. (1991). *Emotion and adaptation*. New York: Oxford University Press.

Lee, R. & Robbins, S. (1995). Measuring belongingness: The social connectedness and social assurance scales. *Journal of Counseling Psychology*, 232-241.

Leonard, K. & Decker, S. (1994, March-April). The theory of social control: Does it apply to the very young? *Journal of Criminal Justice*, 89-105.

Lewis, B. & Yarnell, H. (1951). Pathological firesetting (pyromania). *Nervous & Mental Disease Monographs*, 82.

Libbey, P. & Bybee, R. (1979). The physical abuse of adolescents. *Journal of Social Issues*, 35, 101-126.

Lock, J. (1996). Disruptive behavior disorder. In H. Steiner (Ed.). *Treating adolescents* (43-76). San Francisco: Jossey-Bass.

Loeber, R., Green, S., Keenan, K. & Lahey, B. B. (1995). Which boys will fare worse?: Early predictors of the onset of conduct disorder in a six year longitudinal study. *Journal of American Academy of Child and Adolescent Psychiatry*, 34, 499-509.

Loeber, R. & Schmaling, K. (1985). Empirical evidence for overt and covert patterns of antisocial conduct problems. *Journal of Abnormal Child Psychology*, 13, 337-352.

Loeber, R. & Stouthamer-Loeber, (1986). Family factors as correlates and predictors of juvenile conduct problems and delinquency. In M. Tonry and N. Morris (Eds.), *Crime and Justice: An Annual Review of Research*, 7, 29-149.

Lutzker, J., Bigelow, K., Swenson, C., Doctor, R., & Kessler, M. (1999). Problems related to child abuse and neglect. In S. Netherton, D. Holmes & C.E. Walker (Eds.), *Child & adolescent psychological disorders*. New York: Oxford University Press.

Lykken, D. (1996). Psychopathy, sociopathy, and crime. *Society*, 34, 30-38.

MacDonald, J. (1977). *Bombers and firesetters*. Springfield, IL.: Charles Thomas

Macht, L.B. & Mack, J.E. (1968). The firesetter syndrome. *Psychiatry*, 31, 277-288.

Magee, J. (1933). Pathological arson. *Scientific Monthly*, 37, 358-361.

Maguire, K. & Pastore, A. (1995). *Sourcebook of Criminal Justice Statistics-1994*. Washington, DC: US Department of Justice, Bureau of Justice Statistics.

Maslow, A. (1954). *Motivation and personality*. New York: Harper & Row.

McKerraccher, D. & Dacre, A. (1966). A study of arsonists in a special security hospital. *British Journal of Psychiatry*, 112, 1151-1154.

Maletzsky, B. (1991). *Treating the sexual offender*. Newbury, CA: Sage.

Malone, J. (1990). Schizophrenia research update: Implications for nursing. *Journal of Psychosocial Nursing*, 28 (8), 4-6, 8-9.

Marin, P. (1975, October). The new narcissism. *Harper's*, 45-56.

Maslow, A. (1954). *Motivation and personality*. New York: Harper & Row.

McCord, W. & McCord, J. (1964). *The psychopath*. Princeton, NJ: Van Nostrand.

McGlashan, T. (1989). Schizophrenia: Psychodynamic theories. In H. Kaplan, & B. Sanders (Eds.), *Comprehensive textbook of psychiatry* (5th ed.), Baltimore: Williams & Wilkins.

Meissner, W.W. (1979). Internalization and object relations. *Journal of the American Psychoanalytic Association*, 27, 345-360.

Meltzer, H. (1987). Biological studies in schizophrenia. *Schizophrenia Bulletin*, 13(1), 77-111.

Menard, S. (1995). A development test of Mertonian anomic theory. *Journal of Research in Crime and Delinquency*, 32, 136-174.

Merton, R. (1968). *Social theory and social structure*. (3rd. ed.). New York: Free Press.

Messerschmidt, J. (1986). *Capitalism, patriarchy and crime*. Totowa, NJ: Rowman & Littlefield.

Messner, S. & Rosenfeld, R. (1994). *Crime and the American dream*. Belmont, CA: Wadsworth.

Merton, R. (1968). *Social theory and social structure* (enlarged ed.). New York: Free Press.

Millon, T. (1981). *Disorders of personality-DSM-III: Axis 11*. New York: John Wiley & Sons.

Minuchin, P. (1977). *The middle years of childhood*. Monterey, CA.: Brooks/Cole Publishing.

Mirowsky, J. & Ross, C. (1995). Sex differences in distress: Real or artifact." *American Sociological Review*, 60, 449-468.

Moffitt, T.E. (1990). Juvenile delinquency and attention deficit disorder: Boys' developmental trajectories from age 13 to age 15. *Child Development*, 61, 893-910.

Moffitt, T.E. (1993). Adolescence-limited and life-course-persistent antisocial behavior: A developmental taxonomy. *Psychological Review*, 100, 674-701

Moffitt, T. & Silva, P. (1988). Self-reported delinquency, neuropsychological deficit and history of attention deficit disorder. *Journal of Abnormal Child Psychology*, 16, 553-569.

Monahan, J. (1984). The prediction of violent behavior: Toward a second generation of theory and policy. *American Journal of Psychiatry*, 141, 10-15.

Monahan, J. (1992). Mental disorder and violent behavior: Perceptions and evidence. *American Psychologist*, 47, 511-521.

Monteleone, J. (1994). *Recognition of child abuse for the Mandated Reporter*. New York: Mosby-Year Book.

Moore, D. (Ed.). (1982). *Adolescence and Stress*. Report of NIMH Conference, Washington, DC: US Department of Health and Human Services, Public Health Service.

Morse, A., Hyde, J.N., Newberger, E. & Reed, R. (1977). Environmental correlates of pediatric social illness: Preventive implications of an advocacy approach. *American Journal of Public Health*, 67, 612-615.

Mrazek, P. & Mrazek, D. (1987). Resilience in child maltreatment victims: A conceptual model. *Child Abuse and Neglect*, 11, 357-366.

Muckley, A. (1997). *Firesetting: Addressing fire-setting behavior with children, young people and adults*. London, UK: Arson Prevention Bureau.

Murphy, L. & Moriarity, A. (1976). *Vulnerability, coping, and growth*. New Haven: Yale University Press.

Norton, D. (1993, Dec. 21). Keller charged in 3 arson deaths. *The Seattle Times*, A 1.

Oates, R., Forrest, D. & Peacock, A. (1985). Mothers of abused children. *Clinical Pediatrics*, 24(1), 9-13.

Olweus, D. (1978). *Aggression in the schools: Bullies and whipping boys*. Washington, DC: Hemisphere.

Östman, O. (1991). Child and adolescent psychiatric patients in adulthood. *Acta Psychiatrica Scandanavica*, 84, 40-45.

Panel on moral education. (May, 1988). Moral education in the life of the school. *Educational Leadership*, 4-8.

Papalia, D. & Olds, S. (1995). *Human development* (6th ed.). New York: McGraw-Hill.

Patterson, G., DeBaryshe, B. D. & Ramsey, E. (1989). A developmental perspective on antisocial behavior. *American Psychologist*, 44, 329-335.

Pelton, L. (1979). Interpreting family violence data. *American Journal of Orthopsychiatry*, 49, 372-374.

Piaget, J. (1932). *The moral judgment of the child*. New York: Harcourt Brace Jovanovich.

Piaget, J. (1958). *The growth of logical thinking from childhood to adolescence*. New York: Basic Books.

Pisani, A. (1995, March). *Arson research: A critical review of the literature*. Unpublished manuscript.

Planansky, K. & Johnston, R. (1977). Homicidal aggression in schizophrenic men. *Acta Psychiatrica Scandanavica*, 55, 65-73.

Plomin, R., & Rende, R. (1991). Human behavioral genetics. *Annual Review of Psychology*, Vol. 42. Palo Alto, CA: Annual Reviews, Inc.

Polk, K. & Richmond, L. (1972). Those who fail. In K. Polk & L. Richmond (Eds.), *Schools and delinquency*, (p. 67). Englewood Cliffs, NJ: Prentice-Hall.

Polk, K. & Schafer, W. (Eds.). (1972). *Schools and delinquency*. Englewood Cliffs, NJ: Prentice-Hall.

Porter, S., Fairweather, D., Drugge, J., Herve, H., Birt, A., & Boer, D. (2000). Profiles of psychopathy in incarcerated sexual offenders. *Criminal Justice and Behavior*, 27, 216-233.

Power, D.J. (1969). Subnormality and crime I. *Medical Science Law*, 83-93.

Prentsky, R. & Knight, R. (1991). Identifying critical dimensions for discriminating among rapists. *Journal of Consulting and Clinical Psychology*, 59, 643-691.

Prevent Child Abuse America. *Current trends in child abuse prevention and fatalities: The 2000 fifty state survey*. Chicago, IL.: Author

Quinsey, V., Chaplin, T., & Unfold, D. (1989). Arsonists and sexual arousal to firesetting: Correlations unsupported. *Journal of Behavior Therapy and Experimental Psychiatry*, 20, 203-209.

Rabkin, J. (1979). Criminal behavior of discharged mental patients. *Psychological Bulletin*, 86, 1-27.

Rasnen, P., Puumalainen, T., Janhonen, S. & Vaisenen, E. (1996). Firesetting from the viewpoint of an arsonist. *Journal of Psychosocial Nursing and Mental Health Services*, 34(3), 16-21.

Rathus, S. & Siegal, L. (1973). Delinquent attitudes and self-esteem. *Adolescence*, 7, 265-276.

Ravateheino, J. (1989). Finnish study of 180 arsonists arrested in Helsinki. *Fire Protection*, 223, 30-34.

Reckless, W. (1961). A new theory of delinquency and crime. *Federal Probation*, 25, 42-46.

Reckless, W. (1967). *The crime problem* (4th ed.). New York: Appleton-Century-Crofts.

Reid, J. (1993). Prevention of conduct disorder before and after school entry: Relating interventions to developmental findings. *Development and Psychopathology*, 5, 243-262.

Reid, S. T. (1997). *Crime and Criminology* (8th ed.). Madison, WI: Brown & Benchmark.

Reiss, A. & Rhodes, A. (1961). The distribution of juvenile delinquency in the social class structure. *American Sociological Review*, 26, 720-732.

Reiss, A. & Roth, J.A. (Eds.). (1993). *Understanding and preventing violence.* Washington, DC: National Academy Press.

Rennison, C. A. (2002). *Criminal victimization 2001: Changes 2000-2001 with trends 1993-2001.* Washington, DC: Bureau of Justice Statistics.

Robins, N. L. (1966). *Deviant children grown up.* Baltimore: Williams & Wilkins

Robins, L. N. & McEvoy, L. (1990). Conduct problems as predictors of substance abuse. In L. Robins & M. Rutter (Eds.). *Straight and devious pathways from childhood to adulthood.* Cambridge: Cambridge University Press.

Robinson, M.B. (2002). *Justice Blind? Ideals and realities of American criminal justice.* Upper Saddle River, NJ: Prentice Hall.

Rose, H.M., Maggiore, A., & Schaefer, B. (1998). *The Milwaukee homicide project: Final report.* Unpublished report. Washington, DC.: US Department of Justice, Office of Justice Programs, Office of Juvenile Justice and Delinquency Prevention.

Rosen, L. & Neilson, K. (1982). Broken homes. In L. Savitz & N. Johnson (Eds.), *Contemporary criminology.* New York: J. Wiley.

Russell, D. (1983). The incidence and prevalence of intrafamilial and extrafamilial sexual abuse of female children. *Child Abuse and Neglect*, 17, 133-146.

Rutter, M. (1981). *Maternal deprivation reassessed* (2nd ed.). London: Penguin books.

Rutter, M. (1987). Continuities and discontinuities from infancy. In O.J. Osofsky (Ed.), *Handbook of infant development.* New York: Wiley.

Sakheim, G. & Osborn, E. (1986). A psychological profile of juvenile firesetters in residential treatment: A replication Study. *Child Welfare*, 64(5), 495-503.

Sakheim, G., Vigdor, M., Gordon, M. & Helprin, (1985). A psychological profile of juvenile firesetters in residential treatment: A replication study. *Child Welfare*, 64(5), 494-503.

Santrock, J. (1995). *Life-span development*. Wisconsin: Brown & Little.

Sapsford, R.J., Banks, C. & Smith, D. (1978). *Arsonists in prison: Medicine, science and the law*, 18, 247-254.

Sapp, A., Huff, T., Gary, G., & Icove, D. (1994). *A motive-based offender analysis of serial arsonists*. Washington, DC: National Center for the Analysis of Violent Crime, Federal Bureau of Investigation.

Satterfield, J., Swanson, J., Schell, A., & Lee, F. (1995). Prediction of antisocial behavior in attention-deficit hyperactivity disorder and conduct disorder. *Journal of the American Academy of Child and Adolescent Psychiatry*, 28, 185-190.

Schmalleger, F. (1997). *Criminal justice today* (4th ed.). Upper Saddle River: Prentice Hall.

Schmalleger, F. (2002). *Criminal justice: A brief introduction*. (4th ed. update). Upper Saddle River, NJ: Prentice Hall.

Schmalleger, F. (2004). *Criminal justice: A brief introduction*. (5th ed.). Upper Saddle River, NJ: Pearson Prentice Hall.

Schuckit, M.A. (1998). Biological, psychological, and environmental predictors of alcoholism risk: A longitudinal study. *Journal of Studies on Alcohol*, 59, 485-494.

Schwartz, I.A., Rendon, J., & Hsieh, C-M. (1994, Sept.-Oct.). Is child maltreatment a leading cause of delinquency? *Child Welfare*, 73 (5), 639.

Sealock, M. & Simpson, S. (1998). Unraveling bias in arrest decisions: The role of juvenile offender type-scripts. *Justice Quarterly*, 15, 427-457.

Seidman, L. (1983, September). Schizophrenia and brain dysfunction: An integration of recent neurodiagnostic findings. *Psychological Bulletin*, 94, 195-238.

Shaw, C. & McKay, H.D. (1929). *Delinquency areas*. Chicago: University of Chicago Press.

Shaw, C. & McKay, H. D. (1931). Report on the causes of crime, (2). *Social factors in juvenile delinquency*. Washington, DC: U.S. Government Printing Office.

Shaw, C. & McKay, H.D. (1942). *Juvenile delinquency and urban areas*. Chicago: University of Chicago Press.

Shaw, C. & McKay, H. D. (1969). *Juvenile delinquency and urban areas* (rev. ed.). Chicago: University of Chicago Press.

Showers, J. & Pickrell, E. (1987). Child firesetters: A study of three populations. *Hospital and Community Psychiatry*, 38(5), 495-501.

Siegel, L. (2004). *Criminology: Theories, patterns, & typologies* (8th ed.). Belmont, CA: Wadsworth.

Siegel, L. (2003). *Criminology* (8th ed.). Belmont, CA: Thomson Wadsworth.

Siegel, L. & Senna, J. (1981). *Juvenile delinquency: Theory, practice and law*. New York: West Publishing.

Smith, C. & Thornberry, T. (1995). The relationship between childhood maltreatment and adolescent involvement in delinquency. *Criminology*, 33, 451-481.

Snyder, H. (1999). *Juvenile arrests*, 1997. Office of Juvenile Justice and Delinquency. Washington, DC: U.S. Department of Justice.

Sommers-Flanagan, J. & Sommers-Flanagan, R. (2003). *Clinical interviewing*. (3rd. 3d.). Hoboken, NJ: John Wiley & Sons.

Sosowsky, L. (1986). More on crime among the mentally ill. *American Journal of Psychiatry*, 143, p. 1325.

Spector, R. (1979). *Cultural diversity in health and illness*. New York: Appleton-Century-Crofts.

Stein, A., Freidrich, L. K. (1975). The impact of television on children and youth. In E.M. Hetherington, J. Hagan, R. Kron & A H. Stein (Eds.), *Review of Child Development Research: Vol. 5*. Chicago: University of Chicago Press.

Steiner, H. & Feldman, S. (1996). General principles and special problems. In H. Steiner (Ed.). *Treating adolescents* (1-40). San Francisco: Jossey-Boss.

Stewart, L. (1993, August). Profile of female firesetters: Implications for treatment. *British Journal of Psychiatry*, 163, 248-256.

Straker, N. (1979). Impulse and conduct disorders. In M. Josephson & R. Porter (Eds.). *Clinician's handbook of childhood psychopathology* (351-365). New York: Jason Aronson, Inc.

Sutherland, E. (1947). *Principles of criminology* (4th ed.). Chicago: J.B. Lipponcott.

Sutherland, E. & Creasey, D. (1970). *Criminology* (10th ed.). Philadelphia: Lipponcott.

Swaffer, T. & Hollin, C. (1995). Adolescent firesetting: Why do they say they do it? *Journal of Adolescence*, 18(5). 619-623.

Taylor, P.J. (1998). When symptoms of psychosis drive serious violence. *Social Psychiatry and Psychiatric Epidemiology*, 33, 47-54.

Taylor, P. & Gunn, J. (1984). Violence and psychosis I. Risk of violence among psychotic men. *British Medical Journal of Clinical Research*, 288, 1945-49.

Teplin, L. (1984). Criminalizing mental disorder. *American Psychologist*, 39, 794-803.

Territo, L., Halstead, J. & Bromley, M. (2004). *Crime and justice in America, a human perspective*. Upper Saddle River, NJ: Pearson Prentice Hall.

Thomas, A. & Chess, S. (1984). Genesis and evolution of behavioral disorders: From infancy to early adult life. *American Journal of Orthopsychiatry*, 141(1), 1-9.

Thornberry, T. & Smith, C. (1995).

Thurber, S. & Dahmes, R. (1999). Impulse control disorders not elsewhere classified. In S. Netherton, S. Holmes & C.E. Walker (Eds.), *Child and adolescent psychological disorders* (pp. 439-463). New York: Oxford Press.

Tolan, P.H. & Thomas, P. (1995). The implications of age of onset for delinquency II: Longitudinal data. *Journal of Abnormal Child Psychology*, 23, 157-169.

Torrey, E.F. (1988). *Surviving schizophrenia: A family manual* (rev. ed.). New York: Harper & Row.

Trickett, P. K., Aber, J., Carlson, V., & Cicchetti, D. (1991). Relationships of socioeconomic status to the etiology and development sequelae of physical child abuse. *Developmental Psychology*, 27, 148-158.

Trickett, P. & Susman, E. J. (1988). Parental perceptions of child-rearing practices in physically abusive and non-abusive families. *Developmental Psychology*, 24(2), 270-276.

Unell, B. & Wyckoff, J. (1995). *20 Teachable virtues*. New York: Berkley.

U.S. Bureau of the Census (1996). *Families with children under 18 by type: 1995 to 2010, Series 1, 2, and 3*. Washington, DC.

U.S. Department of Health and Human Services, National Center on Child Abuse and Neglect (1995). *Child maltreatment 1993: Reports from the states to the National Center on Child Abuse and Neglect*. Washington, DC: U.S. Government Printing Office.

U.S. Department of Health and Human Services (2003, April 1). *Child abuse prevention: An overview*. Washington, DC: U.S. Government Printing Office.

U.S. Department of Justice. (2000). *Terrorism in the United States-1998*. Washington, DC: USGPO.

Vandersall, J. & Wiener, J. (1970). *Children who set fires*. Archives of General Psychiatry, 22, 63-71.

Vreeland, R. & Levin, B. (1980). Psychological aspects of firesetting. In D. Canter (Ed.), *Fires and Human Behavior*. Washington, DC: National Bureau of Standards.

Vreeland, R. & Waller, M. (1979). *The psychology of firesetting: A review and appraisal*. Washington, DC: U.S. Government Printing Office.

Wauchope, B. & Straus, M. (1990). Physical punishment and physical abuse of American children: Incident rates by age, gender, and occupational class. In M. Straus & R. Gelles (Eds.), *Physical violence in American families: Risk factors and adaptations to violence in 8,145 families* (pp. 133-148). New Brunswick, NJ: Transaction Books.

Wagner, R., Taylor, D., Wright, J., Sloat, A., Springett, G., Arnold, S., & Weinberg, H. (1994). Substance abuse among the mentally ill. *American Journal of Orthopsychiatry*, 64, 30-38.

Weiner, I. (1981). *Child and adolescent psychopathology*. New York: John Wiley & Sons.

Weinrott, M. & Saylor, M. (1991). Self-report of crimes committed by sex offenders. *Journal of Interpersonal Violence*, 6, 286-300.

Weiss, G. (1990). Hyperactivity in childhood. *New England Journal of Medicine*, 323 (20), 1413-1415.

Wells, K. & Egan, J. (1988). Social learning and systems family therapy for childhood oppositional disorder: Comparative treatment outcome. *Comprehensive Psychiatry*, 29, 138-146.

Wesseley, S., Buchanan, A. & Reed, A. (1993). Acting on delusions. I. Prevalence. *British Journal of Psychiatry*, 163, 69-76.

Whitcomb, D. (2001). Child victimization. In G. Coleman, M. Gaboury, M. Murray, & A. Seymour (Eds.), *National Victim Assistance Academy*. Washington, DC: U.S. Department of Justice.

Widom, C. (1989). The cycle of violence. *Science*, 244, 160-166.

Widom, C. (1995, March). *Victims of childhood sexual abuse-later criminal consequences*. National Institute of Justice. Washington, DC: U.S. Department of Justice, p. 2.

Widom, C. & Maxfield, M. (2001, February). *An update on the 'Cycle of Violence'*. (Research in Brief, p. 1-2). Washington, DC: National Institute of Justice

Williams, D. (1998). *Delinquent and deliberate firesetters in the middle years of childhood and adolescence*. Unpublished Dissertation, Walden University,

Williams, D. (2004). Understanding arson: Subtypes and intervention strategies. In R. Hammer, E. Pagliaro & B. Moynihan (Eds.), *Forensic nursing-A handbook for practice*. New York: Jones & Bartlett.

Wilson, H. & Kneisl, C. (1983). *Psychiatric nursing*. Menlo Park, CA.: Addison-Wesley

Wilson, J.Q. & Herrnstein, R. (1985). *Crime and human nature*. New York: Simon and Schuster.

Wilson, W. (1987). *The truly disadvantaged: The inner-city, the underclass and public policy*. Chicago: University of Chicago Press

Wolfe, D.A. (1985). Child-abusive parents: An empirical view and analysis. *Psychological Bulletin*, 97, 462-582.

Wooden, W. & Berkley, M. (1984). *Children and arson: America's middle class nightmare*. New York: Plenum.

Wolff, S. (1999). Personality disorders. In S. Netherton, D. Holmes & C.E. Walker (Eds.). *Child & adolescent psychological disorders.* (pp. 477-493). New York: Oxford University Press.

Wolfner, G. & Gelles, R. (1993). A profile of violence against children: A national study. *Child Abuse and Neglect* 17, 197-212.

Wulfert, E., Block, J.A., Santa Ana, E., Rodriquez, M., & Colsman, M. (2002). Impulsive choices and problem behaviors in early and late adolescence. *Journal of Personality*, 70, 533-552.

Wurtzer, W. (1995, January 5). Keller family saga destined for tv-parents praise portrayal of arson, anguish as an uplifting message of hope and faith. *The Seattle Times*, A 1.

Yablonsky, H. (1984). *Juvenile delinquency.* (3rd ed.). Boston: Houghton Mifflin.

Yoshikawa, H. (1994). Prevention as cumulative protection: Effects of early familial support and education on chronic delinquency and its risks. *Psychological Bulletin*, 115, 28-54.

Zaslow, J. (2003, June 27). Dangerous games. Medical mystery: Why some children keep setting fires. *The Wall Street Journal.*

Zoccoulillo, M. (1993). Gender and the development of conduct disorder. *Development and Psychopathology*, 5, 65-78.

Zubin, J. (1980). Chronic schizophrenia from the standpoint of vulnerability. In C.F. Baxter & C. Melneckuk (Eds.), *Perspectives in schizophrenia research* (pp. 269-294). New York: Raven Press.

Zuckerman, M. (1991). Sensation seeking: The balance between risk and reward. In L.P. Lipsitt & L.L. Mitnick (Eds.), *Self-regulatory behavior and risk taking: Causes and consequences* (pp. 143-152). Norwood, NJ: Ablex.

Zuckerman, M., Kolin, E., Price, L., & Zoob, I. (1964). Development of a sensation seeking scale. *Journal of Consulting Psychology*, 28, 477-482.

Zuckerman, M. & Neeb, M. (1980). Demographic influences in sensation seeking and expressions of sensation seeking in religion, smoking, and driving habits. *Personality and Individual Differences*, 1, 197-206.

Glossary

aberrant conduct—behavior deviating from the usual or standard.

adjudicated delinquent—formal indentification of status of a youth by the court.

antisocial conduct—behavior deviating sharply from the social norm; engaging in hostile or harmful behavior without regard to consequences.

arson—any willful or malicious burning or attempt to burn, with or without intent to defraud, a dwelling, house, public building, motor vehicle or aircraft, or personal property of another.

Attention Deficit Hyperactive Disorder (ADHD)—has three central behaviors: inattention and distractibility, impulsivity, and excessive motor activity.

conduct disorder—refers to a set of constant behaviors that are socially disapproved. According to the DSM-IV (1994), the primary feature of a conduct disorder is repetitive and persistent behavior that violates others' rights.

curiosity or experimental firesetters—a subtype of firesetters who do not intend to cause harm or damage from malice.

delinquency—conduct that is out of accord with accepted behavior or the law.

delusions—a persistent false psychotic belief regarding the self, or persons or objects outside the self.

deviant behavior—exhibiting conduct that is markedly different from the accepted norm.

177

disordered coping firesetters—a subtype of firesetters who set fires in order to return to a state of emotional equilibrium after experiencing intense anxiety and/or rage.

dysfunctional—impaired or abnormal functioning.

ego—one of the three divisions of the psyche in psychoanalytic theory that serves as the organized conscious mediator between the person and reality especially by functioning both in the perception of and adaptation to reality.

hallucinations—perceptions that are false sensory impressions having no basis in reality.

id—one of the three divisions of the psyche in psychoanalytic theory that is completely unconscious and is the source of psychic energy derived from instinctual needs and drives.

illusions—perceptual distortions of some real external stimuli.

kinesics—body language; the study of the relationship between nonlinguistic body motions and communication.

narcissism—self-love; in excess, it interferes with an ability to relate to others.

Oppositional Defiant Disorder (ODD)—conduct that includes desrespect and hostility towards authority figures, as well as disobedience with rules, temper tantrums and displays of spite, anger, and resentment.

paranoid personality disorder—applying to an individual who experiences pervasive and long-standing suspiciousness. The individual perceives the world in a different way and is constantly alert for clues as to the "real" meaning of verbal or behavioral messages from others.

passive aggressive personality disorder—characterized by aggressive behavior demonstrated in passive ways, such as stubbornness or deliberate stalling.

pathology—the structural and functional deviations from the normal that constitute or characterize disease.

personality disorder—a group of mental disorders affecting the personality, characterized by maladaptive behaviors that last a lifetime.

psychopath—an individual who is unable to experience the feelings of love, sympathy (feelings for), and empathy (feelings about) for other people.

psychophysiological—combining or involving mental and bodily processes.

psychosexual—of or relating to the mental, emotional, and behavioral aspects of sexual development.

psychosis—fundamental derangement characterized by defective or lost contact with reality.

psychosocial—involving both psychological and aspects of mental health.

psychotic—a person who is marked by or affected with a fundamental derangement, characterized by defective or lost contact with reality.

pyromania—an irresistible impulse to start fires.

schizophrenia—a psychotic disorder characterized by loss of contact with the einvironment, by noticeable deterioration in the level of functioning in everyday life, and by disintegration of personality expressed as a disorder of feeling, thought and conduct.

socialization—the process through which a person learns to be a functioning member of society.

sociopath—an individual characterized by asocial or antisocial behavior or a psychopathic personality.

superego—one of the three divisions of the psyche in psychoanalytic theory that is only partly conscious, represents internalization of parental conscience and the rules of society, and functions to reward and punish through a system of moral attitudes, conscience, and a sense of guilt.

thought disorder—a condition in which associations lose their continuity so that thinking becomes bizarre, confused, and incorrect. Individuals suffering from thought disorder experience disturbances in verbal and motor behavior that affect their perceptual skills, thinking abilities, affective responses, and motivation.

thrill seeker arsonist or firesetter—is defined, for the purpose of the text, as an individual who sets fires as a way to experience danger and the sensation of risk.

About the Author

Dian Williams has worked with firesetting behavior since 1974 and made the decision to formalize her business in the early 1980's.

The Federal Government recognizes her as one of six arson research fellows in the United States. Dr. Williams appears with some regularity on local and national television programs and was featured on the Discovery Channel recently as an expert in arson profiling.

Dr. Williams lectures on firesetting behavior throughout the U.S. and abroad. She has functioned as a consultant to the Home Office in the United Kingdom and is currently advising on forensic research into arsonists in Australia. Dr. Williams serves as a consultant to police departments, criminal and juvenile justice agencies, criminal and civil courts, mental health departments, news and print media, attorneys and schools.

Index

W

Y

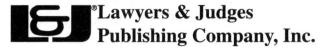

Forensic Aspects of
Chemical and Biological Terrorism, #6672
Cyril H.Wecht, M.D., J.D.

Since the attacks of September 11, 2001, the U.S. has become more aware of its vulnerability to terrorist attacks. Every day our media reports on the possibility of an attack on our soil or an attack on our overseas citizens or military personnel. As terrorist become more determined to cause chaos, the possibility of them using chemical or biological weapons increases. An attack of this nature in any country would pose a great danger to the entire world. *Forensic Aspects of Biological and Chemical Weapons* is an eye-opening resource for healthcare professionals, 911 operators, emergency response personnel, medical examiners, coroners, crime scene investigators, hospital administrators and public health officials. It provides valuable insight into what areas need improvement, what roles each of the responders should have, and how this all can be accomplished. It also extensively covers the investigation of an attack from the signs and symptoms of various diseases and chemical exposure to how the crime scene should be handled. This timely resource is a must have for anyone involved in public health and public safety. 6" × 9", casebound, 450 pages.

Gangs in Court, #6796
Lewis Yablonksy

Gang laws around the nation are drastically extending the prision sentences of criminals who are believed to be gang members. But how do we really know when a crime is gang-related or how involved the perpetrator was in a gang? Youths are often mistakenly identified as gang-members because of where they live and with whom they associate. They are even prosecuted for being in the "wrong place at the wrong time." This mistake can add years to a person's jail time and often sends them away for life. With over fifty years experience working with gang members in and out of prison, Dr. Lewis Yablonsky will introduce you to the gang-world. Through his research he will explain the various types of gangs, gang behavior and the six catagories of gang-members. 6" × 9", softbound.

These and many more useful products are available through our catalog.

For a FREE catalog, write or call:

Lawyers & Judges Publishing Company, Inc.

P.O. Box 30040 • Tucson, Arizona 85751-0040

(800) 209-7109 • FAX (800) 330-8795
e-mail address: sales@lawyersandjudges.com

Find us on the Internet at:
http://www.lawyersandjudges.com